NOT LIKE THAT!

How to build the wrong thing on purpose
instead of the right thing by accident.

Adam L. Coombes

Not Like That!

First edition

ISBN: [to be assigned]

This book uses clinical software as a case study. Company and product specifics have been deliberately abstracted; any resemblance to identifiable systems is incidental.

Contents

Part One:

The Right Thing, Built Wrong

Chapter One: The Wrong Thing

Being wrong is like being *right, but different.*

There is a moment, familiar to anyone who has spent long enough in software delivery, when you realise that everything has gone wrong in a way that was entirely avoidable yet somehow completely inevitable.

For me, that moment arrived, like an unexpectedly wet sock in a dark room, in a car factory in Germany (the moment, not the sock).

At that time I was working for a large, multinational technology company, as a technical architect in the auspiciously named 'Global Architecture Team', although we didn't do much terraforming. I had spent the better part of a year designing a new system for a major automotive manufacturer. Hardware through to application software, architected from scratch, specified carefully, built to requirements, tested, and signed off by the people in the North American head office who had commissioned it. It worked. It did exactly what it was supposed to do. I was, not unreasonably, quite pleased with it.

The factory manager was not pleased. He had not been consulted. He knew what was coming, and he was ready for us.

"So let me understand this," he said, with the particular, Germanic precision of someone who has understood it perfectly and wants to make sure you have too. "You want to rip out my current system, which I might add is working perfectly, and install this new one that I haven't tested and which will get rid of all the things I've done over the last ten years to make us better than the other factories I compete with internally? And you expect me to pay for it? Gentlemen, it has been a pleasure meeting you and showing you round my factory, but I don't think this will be happening, do you?"

He was right. It didn't happen.

The specific quality of that moment is not something you forget. Standing in a senior executive's office demonstrating something that works perfectly, while that same executive explains, with impeccable courtesy, that it is of no interest to him whatsoever and you may leave now. It's memorable.

There is a version of software failure that has a clear blame shape. A deadline missed, a bug that should have been caught, a decision that was obviously wrong in retrospect. That version is uncomfortable but comprehensible. Someone did something wrong.

This didn't have a shape, a culprit, or a scapegoat. It was perfect! Everyone had done their job. The system worked. The factory manager was right to refuse it. The US head office was right to want it. I had built exactly what I'd been asked to build. The failure was not in any of the individual decisions but in the process that connected them, a process that produced a perfectly functioning system for a context that had never been properly understood.

The US head office kept plugging away for another year. The French responded in a similar, but very 'French' way. I wasn't in that meeting. The project was dropped without ceremony.

There is a more uncomfortable version of this story, which I suspect most people in the information technology industry will recognise. Someone in that US head office did ask, at some point, whether the European plants were on board. The question was probably asked of someone who was on board: a regional director, a global IT lead, someone with enough seniority to represent the factories without being in the factories. The answer was almost certainly yes because, when a global initiative comes down from head office with budget attached and executive sponsorship, the answer to "are you on board?" is yes. Until the moment it actually arrives at your door. Or in this case, the factory manager's door, and he had been getting ready.

This isn't dishonesty. It is a rational response to an impossible question. "Do you support the standardisation initiative?" is not the same question as "Will you give up the systems that make your factory more competitive than the others?" The first question gets asked in quarterly reviews. The second only gets asked when someone turns up with a project plan and a timeline (which is, as it turned out, too late).

Requirements processes are almost entirely unprepared for this dynamic. They are good at capturing what people say they want when asked directly. They are not good at surfacing what people will actually do when what they said they wanted arrives.

What strikes me now, thirty-odd years later, is that nobody involved had built the wrong thing on purpose. The US head office wanted standardisation across their global operation: rational. The factory manager wanted to protect ten years of internal competitive advantage: rational. My team had delivered exactly what was specified: rational. The outcome was two years of effort, a perfectly functioning system that was never deployed, and the kind of organisational silence that follows when everyone has agreed not to discuss what just happened.

This is a central problem of software delivery, and it has nothing to do with technology.

The natural instinct when a project fails is to look for the mistake. Someone must have done something wrong. There is a whole industry of post-mortems and lessons learned exercises built on the assumption that failure has a proximate cause that can be identified, addressed, and avoided next time. Experience has taught me that either we don't learn the lessons, or the assumption is wrong. The automotive project didn't fail because of a mistake. It failed because the process we used to build it was structurally incapable of surfacing the information that would have told us it was going to fail. We asked the right questions of the wrong people, in the wrong order, at the wrong stage. The factory manager's position was entirely knowable before the project started. It was just never part of the specification process to find out. In fact I strongly suspect that, had he been asked 'Are you on board?' by a senior executive with an open capex budget, he would have given an unequivocal 'Yes!' and still have kicked us out twelve months later.

This is the pattern. Not incompetence. Not malice. Not even poor project management, particularly. The standard approach to building software (establish the requirements, design the solution, build it, test it, deploy it) contains within it a structural assumption that the people who commission the work and the people who will use it have compatible objectives, and that asking the right questions of the right people will surface any incompatibilities before they become expensive. This assumption is wrong often enough to be worth examining carefully. And remember, it's not usually the business/requirements analyst's job to scupper the project.

The system wasn't wrong because the engineers failed. It was wrong because the people who specified it asked the people who were sponsoring it and paying the bill what they wanted, and the people who actually had to live with it weren't in the room until it was too late to matter. By the time the factory manager delivered his verdict, a year of work had already happened. The specification was complete. The build was done. The only thing left was the rollout (which is exactly when you discover whether you've built the right thing).

This is too late. This is almost always too late. (Unless it's an aeroplane, or especially if it's an aeroplane, depending on your perspective.)

There are domains where discovering the problem at rollout is not an option, and those domains have something in common: completely fixed scope, engineering understanding built up over decades of failure analysis, and absolutely no tolerance for error at any stage, including testing. Aeroplanes. Bridges. Nuclear power stations. I've worked on some of these too, and in those domains, the waterfall methodology (specify everything upfront, build to the specification, test exhaustively before anyone gets near it) is not just appropriate, it is the only rational approach. You do not ship a minimum viable reactor.

Software is not typically nuclear. The scope is likely to vary, the understanding is not complete, and the cost of discovering you've built the wrong thing, while often significant, is rarely measured in fatalities. There is also a subtler version of this difference that is worth naming. In domains where the specification really can be complete, the gap between what was specified and what was built is a quality problem: did the build match the specification? If it did, and the specification was correct, the thing works. Software's gap is different. The specification is almost never complete, because the people who wrote it could not know everything they needed to know at the time they wrote it. The people who will use the system learn what they actually need from seeing what they don't have. Which means the gap between what was specified and what was needed is not a quality problem. It is a knowledge problem. And knowledge problems do not get solved by more rigorous specification. They get solved by getting the right information in front of the right people at the right time.

Which brings us back to that factory in Germany. And to the question this book tries to answer: how do you find out you've built the wrong thing before you've built it?

Who this is for

Product managers and product owners, business analysts, delivery leads, the more experienced developers, and the domain specialists who know things the software will need and can rarely write down, and senior leaders who want an insight into how their teams might be changing soon. The clinical material is what makes the book's hardest examples hard, but this is not a healthcare-software book. If it works where a distracted registrar meets an intransigent system 10 hours into an 8-hour late shift, it works for your boiler-quote engine and your logistics dashboard too. The setting is medicine because medicine is unforgiving; the argument is about software of any kind that has to meet real people doing real work.

Chapter Two: The Specification Illusion

A perfectly drawn outline doesn't make a murder, ask any crow.

There is something seductive about a requirements document. It has the appearance of certainty (bullet points, version numbers, sign-offs, a date at the top suggesting that a conversation happened, conclusions were reached, and the important decisions recorded for posterity). It is, in most cases, a reasonable interpretation of a photograph of a conversation that happened at a particular time, between particular people, who could only express what they could see or imagine.

I used to genuinely enjoy writing them, 'Customer Wants and Needs', 'Solution Outline Design', 'Business Requirements Document', and more. A good one felt like a real achievement, something solid produced from the fog of stakeholder conversations and competing priorities, something you could hand across a desk and say: build this. My hubris implied that the hard work of understanding what needed to be built had been done. What remained was merely the building, and that was now, satisfyingly, someone else's problem. I don't think about it that way anymore but, for a long time, I was very happy to follow that pattern.

The gap between what the document implies and what it actually is, is the subject of this chapter.

I learned this properly, and expensively, around 2003, from a pension. Stakeholder pensions were new then, and they came with a rule of admirable simplicity: you could not charge the holder more than one percent a year. One number. It is the sort of requirement a regulator can write on a single line and a minister can say out loud, and on the page it is beyond argument.

It is also, as the industry discovered, very close to impossible to obey. The one percent was a specification, and reality (in the form of unit prices, fund switches, and a stock market that has never once paused to consult a regulation before moving), declined to comply. You could charge correctly on Monday and be fractionally over by Friday through nobody's fault at all. So to stay inside the rule you could not simply charge properly and move on. You had to go back, periodically, through every account, reconstruct every transfer, investment and charge, find the points at which the holder had been overcharged, and then perform a modest act of financial time travel: assume the overcharge had never happened, and work out what their position would have been had that money been invested as it should have been. A counter-factual pseudo-reality, computed per customer, across a great many customers. The one percent, you will have noticed, was itself a specification, serenely indifferent to the fact that funds and markets decline to move in tidy single figures. It described the shape of the outcome it wanted and trusted that writing it down would be enough. It wasn't, which is the entire reason my project existed.

My job was to document all of it: the system behaviours that would do the reconstructing, and the customer communications that would explain it. And here is the part that matters. Both were finite. This was not one of those problems where the requirements retreat as you approach them. Every variation could be enumerated. Every condition had a defined, correct, defensible behaviour. It was genuinely complex, but it was bounded, knowable, and documentable, which is to say it was exactly the kind of problem a requirements document is supposed to be good at. If the specification illusion can catch you here, it can catch you anywhere.

So I documented it, and I enjoyed it. The interpolations and extrapolations alone were a pleasure to pin down, the sort of thing that needs a flowchart, and then needs a better flowchart, and some maths. The letters were harder, though not technically: one to tell each holder what we were going to do and why, and a second to follow up with what we had done and what they could do if they were unhappy about it. Those went through far more rounds with legal, marketing and customer communications than I had bargained for, and came out the other end as a genuinely good set of templates, sanded smooth by everyone who had been made to touch them.

I delivered the lot. A full Detailed Business Requirements document. A Detailed Solution Design. A suite of appendices with every letter template in it. It was, and I will own the retrospective wince, rather good. Everyone was very impressed.

Two weeks later I followed up, in the way you do, to ask whether anything needed changing. That was when I learned that the business had brought in a senior consultant. He had insurance and actuarial experience and a daily rate that made my entire engagement look like a rounding error, which, given the subject matter, at least had a certain poetic justice to it. He had spent a month or two not reading my document but talking: to the admin teams who actually ran the systems the pensions lived on, and then to the senior executives, with whom he had agreed an approach. He had rewritten my letters. He had ignored everything else.

I got on with him perfectly well, as it happens. We simply never quite understood one another. I have said, more than once, that I am a mathematician and not an accountant, and that these are not the same thing merely because they both involve numbers. A mathematician wants the structure to be correct: every case handled, the logic sound, the proof closing cleanly. An accountant wants the thing to reconcile in the world: the books to balance, the approach to be one that real admin teams will actually run and real executives will actually sign. He was, unmistakably, an accountant. I had written a beautiful proof. He had gone and found out what would reconcile the business with the customers.

I was made redundant not long afterwards. In hindsight it did me a favour, though it took a while to feel like anything other than the market offering a frank opinion of my flowcharts. I had drawn, if I say so myself, an immaculate outline. Someone else had gone and found out about the murder.

The thing worth sitting with is that the document was not wrong. It was complete, it was correct, and it was admired. Every flowchart would have survived an audit. It simply was not the thing. The specification illusion is the belief that documenting the shape of a thing completely describes the thing. It doesn't. You can specify a bounded problem perfectly and still produce something beside the point, because a document answers the question as it was asked, on the day it was asked, by the people who were in the room to ask it. The organisation had moved the question while I was busy answering it beautifully.

Notice what the consultant actually did. He did not write a better document (or any as far as I could tell). He had conversations, with the people who held the operational knowledge and the people who held the authority, and out of those conversations he assembled something everyone would stand behind. The deciding instrument was never going to be a specification, however good. It was going to be an agreement, and you do not reach an agreement by handing people a binder.

And there is a second pattern, quieter than the first. Notice what survived and what didn't. The system behaviours, the part I had produced more or less alone, were set aside. The letters, the part that had been argued over by legal and marketing and communications until they were right, came through almost untouched. The difference was not quality; my flowcharts were, if anything, the more rigorous artefact. The difference was that the letters had already been reacted to, over and over, by people who could see what was wrong with them. The specification had been reacted to by no one. It had only been admired. I will leave that observation there for now, because it turns out to be most of the rest of this book.

None of this is a failure of effort, or of rigour, or of writing things down. It is simply what writing things down can and cannot do. A requirements document captures what was articulable, by the people present, in the language available to them, on that particular day. The gap between that and what is actually needed is not closed by writing more carefully. Write more carefully and all you have is a more careful record of the same conversation.

The obvious response is to fix the writing. Better requirements. More comprehensive workshops. More rigorous sign-off. A sharper photograph, taken with a better camera, by more people, until the document is so complete that the gap has nowhere left to hide.

I'll talk about the fallacy hidden in that response next.

Chapter Three: Agile Just Made It Faster

The universe is far too busy happening to care how well you've defined it.

I remember the moment I first properly understood Agile development ('Agile requirements management' specifically) and the relief was palpable. It was as though the software industry had finally stopped trying to fight the universe and decided to go with the flow.

In *almost* every project (not just software), requirements change as you work on it: stop pretending they don't. Users don't know what they want until they see it: stop asking them to imagine it. Build something, show it, learn from what happens, adjust. It was obvious, once someone said it out loud, and it felt like my chosen career path had grown up.

To be clear, I started my 'requirements' career defining waterfall processes and waterfall software development lifecycles for the aforementioned global architecture team at the consultancy which no longer exists (I don't think it was a causal relationship). Later, I had been working with some IBM consultants for a while and was at the time very impressed with what they'd done with the Rational Unified Process (RUP) and Unified Modelling Language (UML), but it felt a bit over-engineered.

This may well explain my enthusiasm for Agile when it arrived. I was converted. Genuinely, enthusiastically, without reservation. The relief was real. The promise felt enormous.

The promise was also, it turned out, incomplete. Not wrong (Agile fixed several things that genuinely needed fixing) but aimed at a different problem than the one I'd been struggling with. It took me longer than I'd like to admit to understand the difference.

The Agile Manifesto was written in 2001 by people who had genuinely identified a real problem: waterfall development was too rigid, too slow to respond to change, too committed to a plan written before anyone had built anything. Even RUP was just little waterfalls cascading gently into one another. The solution Agile proposed (iterative development, working software over comprehensive documentation, responding to change over following a plan) was a genuine improvement on what came before.

They were right about a lot of it and, to be fair to Agile, it fixed several things that genuinely needed fixing. The feedback loop shortened. The delivery cadence improved. Progress became visible in a way that "we're still in the requirements phase" never quite managed. A sprint review every two weeks is measurably better and carries less error than a deployment eighteen months after the requirements were signed off.

In an Agile project, the sprint review typically happens somewhere between weekly and every three weeks, depending on how you've decided to implement it (If you've gone for four-weekly or monthly, that's just RUP in a mountain-goat costume). The discovery that you have been building the wrong thing still happens. It just happens sooner, and with less sunk cost. These are real improvements, and the people who designed the approach deserve huge credit for them.

But Agile has three problems that the methodology itself cannot reach, and understanding them is important, because they apply, in different degrees, to almost every iterative approach that followed.

The first is the cost of the material. Every sprint produces production-quality software. Properly engineered, properly tested, properly integrated into the codebase, 'Shippable product'. When the sprint review reveals that something needs to change (and it will, because that is the point of the sprint review) the change is made to production-quality code. The rework is expensive (a lot less expensive than waterfall admittedly, but expensive still), not because the developers are slow or the process is inefficient, but because the material itself is expensive to work with. You are doing discovery work (finding out what you actually need) with the most costly possible tool. A surgeon should not be learning how to excise a tumour on a living person. The analogy is imperfect, but the principle holds: discovery should happen before you commit to expensive material, not during.

The second problem is one of wholeness. Each sprint delivers a piece of the solution: a feature, a workflow, a screen. The sprint review shows that piece. Stakeholders react to that piece. This sounds like progress, and it is, but it carries a hidden cost: nobody sees the whole system until the end (still). And users do not experience software as a collection of pieces delivered in two-week increments. They experience it as a whole, and their reaction to the complete system is qualitatively and quantitatively different from the sum of their reactions to individual features. The Gestalt principle (the whole is greater than the sum of its parts) does not stop applying simply because you've chosen an iterative methodology. A sprint review shows you whether the piece is right. It cannot tell you whether the whole will work. That question remains unanswered until the end, which is precisely where waterfall left it. Minimum viable products (MVPs) help, but only so much. I've heard the discussion too many times, frankly, "Is it minimum viable or minimum valuable, or lovable? And what good is the minimum viable, I don't want the scooter, I want the car!"

The third problem is the deepest. Sprint reviews are good at surfacing feature-level problems: this screen is confusing, this workflow doesn't match how we actually work, this field should be optional not mandatory. They are not good at surfacing premise-level problems. The factory manager's objection in Chapter One was not about a feature. It was about the fundamental premise of the project: that standardisation was desirable, that his factory would benefit from it, that the disruption was worth the gain. No sprint review would have surfaced that objection, because the factory manager was not in the sprint reviews. And if he had been, seeing one feature at a time would not have provoked the reaction that the complete system did. You cannot react to what a thing is until you can see the whole thing. By the time even an Agile project shows you the whole thing, a great deal of production-quality software has been written. In some senses it's worse, because lots of people have already ratified each piece in the sprint reviews, so they have credence.

What unites all three problems is that they stem from a single assumption: that building is the only way to discover. If you accept that assumption, Agile is a significant improvement on waterfall: you discover faster, course correct more frequently, and arrive at something closer to right with less wasted time. But the assumption itself is worth questioning. What if discovery and building were separable? What if you could do your discovery with cheap, throwaway material (something built specifically to provoke reactions, not to survive them) and only commit to production-quality code once you knew what you were building?

The industry has tried a number of approaches, and it is worth briefly acknowledging the ones that came before and after Agile, because the pattern is instructive. Waterfall gave us comprehensive documentation and missed deployments. RAD gave us rapid iterations and scope creep. RUP gave us phases and artefacts and a career opportunity for people who enjoyed drawing process diagrams. XP gave us pair programming and test-driven development. Scrum gave us ceremonies and sprints and the daily stand-up, which is the meeting everyone attends and nobody quite believes is the reason anything gets delivered. SAFe gave us Enterprise Agile, which is what you get when a large organisation decides to implement Agile at scale and the result looks, from certain angles, remarkably like the waterfall it was supposed to replace, only with more meetings and a vocabulary that requires a certification to use correctly.

Each of these addressed real problems. Each of them improved things at the margins. None of them questioned the assumption that building and discovery happen together, with the same material, at the same time.

The reason the methodology keeps changing is that each new one looks like it is addressing the root cause. Waterfall's failure looked like rigidity, so Agile fixed rigidity. Agile's failure at scale looked like a coordination problem, so SAFe fixed coordination. The next methodology will address whatever the current one appears to be failing at. The underlying assumption will persist, unexamined, because it is not visible from inside any methodology. You can only see it by stepping outside and asking what every methodology takes for granted.

What every software methodology takes for granted is that the people doing the specifying have access to the information needed to specify correctly, and that building is the mechanism by which you find out when they don't. The methodologies differ in how frequently they surface that information and how expensive the correction is when they do. None of them ask whether the building itself could be deferred until the information problem is resolved.

That question is the subject of Part Two. But before we get to the answer, there is one more layer of the problem to examine, because the information problem turns out to be even more fundamental than the methodology can see, for reasons that have nothing to do with process and everything to do with how human expertise actually works.

Chapter Four: Schrödinger's Requirement

A requirement is both perfectly understood and completely unknown, until someone's holding a stake

There is a concept in the philosophy of mind called tacit knowledge, and it was described most cleanly by the chemist and philosopher Michael Polanyi in 1966: "We can know more than we can tell." It sounds like a simple observation. It is, on reflection, a fairly serious problem for anyone whose job involves asking people what they know.

Tacit knowledge is the kind you cannot fully articulate. How to ride a bicycle. How to recognise a face. How to know, as an experienced nurse, that a patient is deteriorating before the monitors show it. You have the knowledge. You use it constantly. But if someone asks you to describe it precisely enough that another person could apply it without ever having had the experience, you find yourself reaching for inadequate words, oversimplified rules, and the increasingly unsatisfying phrase "you just know."

This is not a communication failure. It is not a failure of intelligence or effort or professional capability. It is how expertise works. The knowledge becomes tacit precisely because it has been internalised through practice and enhanced through experience (it has moved from conscious, articulable procedure into something faster and more automatic, something that operates below the level at which language can easily reach it). Asking an expert to articulate their tacit knowledge is a bit like asking someone to describe how they balance on a bicycle while they are sitting still. They can tell you some things. They cannot tell you everything. And the things they cannot tell you are often the most important ones.

In the late 1990s I was managing IT for a fuel distributor in East Anglia: agricultural and domestic customers across a large rural area, lorries going out loaded with heating oil and farm diesel, printed delivery schedules that couldn't be changed once the driver had left, delivery notes that occasionally went missing in ways that defied investigation. (One driver maintained for some time that a goat had eaten his. I eventually concluded he was probably right.) We decided to route vehicles using an early neural-network model (the kind based on energy levels in physical networks, designed to find the lowest-energy path through a set of delivery points given the available vehicles, their load compartments, and the road network). It was, in the terminology of computational complexity, an NP-hard problem: one of a class of problems so complex that no known algorithm can solve them efficiently as they scale. We didn't know this at the time. We found out the hard way.

What we proved, after considerable effort and expense, was that the staff in the routing office could do in an hour (with a map, a printed list, and a box of coloured pins) what the computer would take longer than the heat death of the universe to solve. And they wouldn't send a lorry over a non-existent bridge either.

That last detail is the important one. The routing staff knew the roads. Not in the abstract, algorithmic sense that a map encodes them, but in the lived, experiential sense of people who had been driving and routing deliveries across those roads for years. They knew which bridge had a weight restriction that wasn't on any official record, or in one case simply wasn't there anymore. They knew which farm track was impassable in February. They knew which customers could be combined into a single run and which ones were so difficult to access that they needed a particular vehicle (we had some with both front and rear-wheel steering). They knew things that had never been written down, because they had never needed to be written down: the knowledge lived in the people, and the people were in the office (although if I'd referred to them at the time as a living ensemble method I might have got thrown in the loading bay).

When we tried to specify the routing problem formally enough to give it to a computer, we discovered that the formal specification was incomplete in ways we hadn't anticipated and couldn't easily remedy. We could encode the road network. We could encode the vehicle constraints. We could encode the delivery addresses. We couldn't encode a career of knowing where and in which field a particular farmer kept the bowser, and if it shared it with a bull. That knowledge was tacit, and it resisted our best efforts to make it explicit.

This is the problem that requirements workshops are trying to solve, and it is the problem they are structurally least equipped to address. A requirements workshop asks domain experts to sit in a room and describe what they need. To articulate, in advance, the requirements for a system that doesn't exist yet, in language that will be precise enough for an engineer to build from. It assumes that the knowledge exists in an articulable form, waiting to be drawn out by the right questions. Often it doesn't. The knowledge exists, but in a form that can only be expressed through reaction, through seeing something and responding to it, through having an experience and being able to say what was wrong about it.

The routing clerk who answers the question, 'Why is that red pin out there?' with, 'Because of that green pin there and the other red one above it.' The cardiologist who looks at a results display and says 'that's not how I'd expect it?' They're not failing to communicate. They are communicating perfectly (expressing exactly what they know, in the only form that knowledge takes). The problem is that this form of communication requires something to react to. In a requirements workshop, there is often nothing to react to, or at best a PowerPoint. There is only a conversation about a hypothetical future system, and the knowledge that would make that conversation useful is the knowledge that can't survive the translation into words.

Expertise, counterintuitively, can make this worse rather than better. The more deeply someone knows a domain, the harder it often is for them to articulate what they know, because the knowledge has been so thoroughly internalised that it no longer presents itself as separable facts. The routing staff couldn't tell you everything they knew about the road network, not because they were inarticulate but because they had stopped thinking about it as discrete items of knowledge. It had become intuition. And intuition, by definition, does not come with a source citation or a specification document.

I learned something about this from years of running requirements elicitation workshops, and it was a lesson I arrived at mostly by accident. I developed a habit of keeping a whiteboard or a flipchart in the room, and at certain moments in the conversation (when the talking was becoming circular, when people were retreating into abstractions, when I could feel the room losing confidence in its own ability to say anything useful) I would throw the pen to someone and tell them to get on with it. Draw what you mean. Show me the workflow. Put the problem on the board.

It worked, consistently, in ways that surprised me. People who had been struggling to find words would pick up the pen and produce something (rough, usually; approximate, often; sometimes genuinely terrible as a piece of draughtsmanship) and the room would immediately have something to react to. Not a perfect articulation of the requirement, but something close enough to 'wrong' that the corrections started flowing. "No, not like that, more like this." The pen would move to someone else. The drawing would change. Suddenly, I'd need more pens. The knowledge that had been locked behind language would begin, slowly, to surface.

I think, in retrospect, that I had stumbled onto a very manual, very human form of prototyping. The drawing was a prototype. The reaction to the drawing was the requirement. The process of correction and adjustment was, in miniature, exactly the process this book is going to argue for at much greater scale and with considerably better tools. The insight is not new. Good facilitators have been discovering it independently for decades, whenever they got frustrated enough with the talking to pick up a pen.

What this tells us (and it is the conclusion that Part One has been building toward) is that the information problem is not a process problem. It cannot be fixed by better questioning, more comprehensive workshops, or more rigorous documentation. It cannot be fixed by a methodology that relies on people articulating what they need before they have seen anything to react to, or one, however iterative, that only shows pieces of the puzzle without the picture. The knowledge that matters most is the knowledge that only becomes expressible in response to something real.

The question is what to do about that. And the answer, which will feel counterintuitive until you try it, is the subject of Part Two.

Part Two: Build the Wrong Thing on Purpose

Chapter Five: Build It Anyway

No-one Expected The Chain Of Custody!

Part One established three things. First, that the gap between what gets specified and what is actually needed is structural. It's partly a feature of how specification works and partly down to the challenge us humans face when trying to improvise. Second, that no methodology has fixed this, because the methodologies have addressed the symptoms rather than the cause, and the cause is more fundamental than a process can reach. Third, that the knowledge which would close the gap is tacit. It exists in domain experts, but in a form that only becomes expressible in response to something real.

The answer that follows from these three things is counterintuitive. It will feel, on first encounter, like it cannot possibly be right: Build the wrong thing on purpose.

Not accidentally, as has been happening throughout the history of software development. Deliberately. Build something you know is not the final product, built from material you intend to throw away, for the explicit purpose of giving the people who will use it something real enough to react to. Build it not to be wrong, but knowing it will be, so that the wrongness can be found cheaply. Build it before you build the real thing, so that the real thing benefits from everything the wrong thing taught you.

This is a prototype. Not a proof of concept in the traditional sense (a demonstration that something is technically possible) but a question, realised not to survive but to provoke.

Some years ago I was working on a new case management system for the police service. The technical basis was a CRM platform, which meant that building convincing mock screens, not production software but functional enough to be worth showing, took a few days per screen rather than the weeks it would have taken to build from scratch. This was a sustainable order of magnitude as the people running the project were (another) well-known consulting firm who would just add it to the bill. We had the budget and appetite to use the screens as a discovery tool, and we produced a series of them representing the workflow for booking in a suspect and capturing and storing evidence.

We showed the screens to a detective chief inspector. He was experienced, straightforward, and not especially interested in indulging us because the subject matter does not benefit from frivolity. He looked at what we had built and said, with complete sincerity: "I hate it."

This was, in every meaningful sense, the best possible outcome.

What followed was a stream of questions that no requirements document had anticipated and no workshop had surfaced. How do I know what the buttons do? Why are the colours like this? How do I find out who else has looked at this record? And then, the one that stopped the room: where is the chain of custody information captured?

At the time I didn't know what a chain of custody was. I said so. The detective looked at me with the expression of a man who has just been told that someone has built him a car without wheels and seems puzzled by his reaction. Chain of custody (the unbroken record of who has handled evidence, when, and under what authority) is not an optional feature in police case management. It is the mechanism by which evidence is kept admissible. Without it, a case can collapse at trial regardless of what the investigation found. It is foundational, non-negotiable, and so completely obvious to everyone who works in that environment that the possibility of its absence had simply never occurred to anyone to mention.

My admission that I had no idea what a chain of custody was became the seed for another workshop and another module. The module was not in the original scope. It was not in the original budget. It was not in any conversation that preceded the prototype session. It existed in the detective's professional world as completely and obviously as gravity, which meant it was the last thing he would ever have thought to specify.

The screen had to be wrong before he could tell us it was wrong. That was not a problem with the screen. That was the screen doing exactly what it was built to do.

Our project manager had been exercised about the apparent lack of progress. The requirements sessions up to that point looked, from the outside, like a lot of conversation and not much delivery. He attended the detective's session and left in an excellent mood. The volume of feedback, the detail of the reactions, the chain of custody discussion: all of it, in his view, was a sign we were getting somewhere.

We weren't getting anywhere in any sense he would have recognised as progress. We were finding out what we should have found out before we started building, at a point in the project when the cost of finding out was still manageable. What looked like a productive meeting was actually a controlled demolition of several weeks of work. The difference between a controlled demolition and an uncontrolled one is that you choose when it happens.

I left the project a few months later. Whether the chain of custody module made it into the final system I cannot tell you. But I know it was in the requirements.

None of this is a new idea. Prototyping has been part of the software development vocabulary for decades, and the principle, build something rough, show it, learn from the response, has been understood in various forms for as long as people have been designing things for other people to use. It has respectable modern names, too: dual-track development, design thinking, Lean UX, user-centred design, the discovery and alpha phases in the government's own service manual, specification by example, the behaviour-driven development this book leans on later. If your instinct is that you already do a version of this, you are right, and I am not going to pretend otherwise. The problem, for most of that time, was not the idea but the cost.

I had that conversation explicitly, working at a laboratory software company. We were deciding whether to prototype a new clinical workflow before committing to a full build. By the time you had built something convincing enough to generate useful reactions from clinical users, something with real screens, real navigation, something that felt like software rather than a collection of boxes on a diagram, you had spent most of the effort it would take to build the actual thing. The prototype would be thrown away (and in fact, in the current state of the art, MUST be thrown away, more on that later). The learning was real but the overhead was significant, and on a project with a fixed budget and a committed timeline, the case for prototyping was difficult to make against the case for just getting on with it. The police CRM worked because the underlying platform reduced the cost of building mock screens to days rather than weeks. That was the exception. For most projects, in most contexts, the economics were against it.

Cost was the main barrier, but not the only one. Even where a team could afford to prototype, the habit was hard to make stick. I once led a large insurer's transformation to design thinking, and watched it half-succeed: the thinking took and did real good, but the heavy UML notation it arrived wrapped in did not, because it was one more formal language to train several hundred people in, the same over-engineering I'd admired and distrusted back in Chapter Three. The method worked; the ceremony around it was the tax nobody kept paying. And the ceremony kept coming back to the same root: a prototype had to be built by a developer, the scarcest and most fought-over person in the building, so 'let's prototype it first' competed with the sprint, and the sprint usually won.

What has changed, and this is what makes the argument in this book practically possible rather than theoretically appealing, is the cost of the material.

AI-assisted development tools have collapsed the time required to build a working prototype from weeks to days, and from days to hours for simpler workflows. I am not a programmer. I have never been a programmer, at least not professionally. For most of my career, this meant that building a prototype was something I either had to commission from an engineer (which put it back on the budget and timeline where the cost objection applied) or approximate with tools that produced something close enough to a wireframe, so that domain experts looked at it and saw a diagram rather than software. Neither was ideal. The former was expensive. The latter provoked reactions to the drawing rather than to the thing.

Working on the prototype that preceded this book, I built a functioning clinical application, real screens, real navigation, real data interactions, in a modern development framework, without writing a line of code. On my own, in days, not weeks. Built to be shown, not built to survive. Built using just conversational descriptions and pictures of the UI, from the specific clinical context I had been working in, detailed enough that a clinician looking at it would see software, not a mockup. The reactions I got were the reactions of someone encountering a real system, which meant they were the reactions that contained real requirements.

That is the game changer. Not the idea of prototyping, which is old. The collapse of the material cost, which is new. When building the wrong thing costs a fraction of what building the right thing costs, the economics of the argument change entirely. The overhead disappears. The learning remains. The case for prototyping, which was always strong in principle, becomes irresistible in practice.

A prototype, properly understood, has three properties that distinguish it from everything else in the development process.

It is whole. Unlike a sprint delivery, which shows one piece of the system, a prototype shows the complete experience, the flow, the navigation, the feel of the thing as a system rather than a collection of features. The detective who looked at the evidence capture screen was looking at it in context, having navigated to it through a workflow that felt recognisably like his workflow. His reaction was the reaction of someone encountering a complete idea, not a fragment. That is why it surfaced requirements that sprint reviews never would.

It is cheap. The material is designed to be discarded. There is no sunk cost in being wrong, because the cost of being wrong was budgeted from the start, which means our reaction to criticism changes. When the detective said "I hate it," my response was not a defence of the work, it was to reach for a notebook.

It is a question. Not "here is what we have built" but "here is what we think you need. Are we right?" The posture it creates is different. A sprint review shows deliverables. A prototype session opens a conversation. The expert is not being asked to evaluate work; they are being asked to react to a hypothesis. "I hate it" is not a failure. "I hate it" is data.

Who you show it to, and how you run the session, are the subjects of the next two chapters.

Chapter Six: Who's In the Room

Nice demo, thanks for all the sandwiches.

There is a dependable way to find out who should have been in the room: build the thing without them, ship it, and wait. It works every time. It is also (possibly) one of the most expensive diagnostic instruments ever devised. This chapter is about a cheaper one.

I'll start back at the laboratory software company, where I also baby-sat what was then the most widely used clinical order communications system in the NHS. We carried the orders and results for nearly every system in secondary care, which meant we held something close to a real-time picture of every patient's diagnostic activity in a hospital. The obvious product, and everyone agreed it was obvious, was a ward display. A large or handheld screen to sit alongside the physical whiteboards (note this for later) on the wards, showing every patient in every bed: latest results, outstanding orders, alerts, colour coded by result status and specialty. It was location sensitive. A clinician could walk onto another ward, tap their mobile device on a tag, and see the patients in front of them, or keep 'their' patients on a separate board entirely. If a patient had been moved to another ward, the board knew. If they were temporarily off the ward having a CT scan, the board knew that too. You could read a patient's NEWS score from across the room. All of it in real time.

We did a lot of work to get it ready. Months of it. Demonstration sessions with our sales and services teams, some of whom had clinical backgrounds. Long conversations with operational managers, who were enthusiastic, because patient flow (how patients move through A&E, the acute units and the inpatient wards, and eventually out of the door) is the problem that keeps hospital managers awake at night, and beds are the scarcest resource in the building. Conversations with doctors about what they needed to know about a patient's results. PowerPoint mock-ups, refined and refined again. Everyone thought it was great. We built it.

Eventually I managed to get an audience with the nurses who would actually use it. We called it a lunch and learn. In the event, the learning was all mine.

They slated it. (You may be detecting a theme by now. That theme is, more or less, this book.)

Their objection was not that it didn't work. It was that it didn't help. They already had whiteboards: physical ones (told you), sectioned up to match the layout of the ward, written and drawn on freehand as the day demanded. Those boards ran shift handover. They were the communications hub of the ward. Yes, our system might know things they had missed or weren't privy to (a house doctor discreetly ordering tests was the canonical example), but they were busy enough already, they had processes for exactly that, and since much of the surrounding workflow still ran on paper they would probably hear about it when the doctor rang the lab anyway. They didn't like the layout. They didn't like the scrolling. The colour coding was at odds with the conventions of their other systems, which, they pointed out, might actively confuse people. And then the detail that has stayed with me ever since: a lot of patient moves were only entered into the EPR at shift change. Our proudly real-time board would have spent much of the day displaying, with great confidence and at considerable expense, a fiction.

We scrapped the product.

Consider who had been in the room for those months. Sales and services colleagues with clinical backgrounds: clinical familiarity, but not current operational knowledge. Operational managers: a real problem, flow and beds, but they would never stand in front of the board at a handover. Doctors: genuine consumers of results and generators of paper, but not the owners of the ward's information ecosystem. Every one of those conversations was useful, and every one of those people was acting in good faith. None of them was a ward nurse. The ward nurses, once finally asked, took about an hour over sandwiches to tell us what months of refinement had not.

There is a deeper reason the right people matter, beyond remembering to invite them. The person who has done a job longest is the one you most need in the room, and also the hardest to get a useful reaction from. A clinician who has spent half a lifetime reviewing results has the right expertise, but it has become so thoroughly internalised that they have largely stopped noticing what they know. The question is not whether they can tell you what is wrong with the prototype. They can, absolutely, and they will. The question is whether they will tell you the things that are so obvious to them that it has never occurred to them to mention them.

Chain of custody in a police case management system. The bridge that every lorry driver in East Anglia knows doesn't take heavy goods vehicles but that never made it onto any official map. The knowledge that the prototype will surface is the knowledge that didn't make it into the specification, because the people who wrote the specification are rarely the people who hold it, and if they are they rarely realise it.

There is a version of this problem that presents as a question about hierarchy: the person who commissioned the project versus the person who will use it. Budget authority versus operational knowledge. These are almost never the same person. The person with budget authority can tell you what they want built. The person with operational knowledge can tell you whether it will work. Showing the prototype to one of them and drawing conclusions that apply to the other is one of the more reliable ways to end up with a finished system that is exactly what was asked for and completely unusable in practice. You need both to crystallise out the value.

The more interesting version of the problem is the one where you have the right person in the room but the wrong conditions. A nurse in a requirements meeting, removed from the ward, asked to describe a workflow in the abstract, is not in the same cognitive state as a nurse on a ward at eleven on a Tuesday with three patients who need reviewing and a system that is about to present them with results for a patient they're not currently looking at. The context in which expertise operates is part of the expertise. A prototype session gets you closer to the right context than a workshop, but it doesn't get you all the way there.

What it does do, if the right people are in the room, is give the expertise something to react to. The nurse who cannot describe in the abstract what they need from a results display will tell you exactly what is wrong with the one you've built them, in specific and immediately actionable terms, the moment you put it in front of them. The problem is that they're mid-shift on a ward, and getting them into a room to look at a prototype requires someone to decide that their time is worth the project's.

That decision is where most prototype sessions go wrong. Not in the method. Not in the prototype. In the room.

The people who should be there are busy doing the actual job, and junior enough that the sponsor is not sure they count. So the sponsor decides, in complete good faith, that he can represent them himself, or that their manager can, or that a quick survey will do it. He cannot. It won't. A manager knows what the team does; a survey tells you what people say; neither is a nurse at the whiteboard at shift handover explaining that the board you propose to replace is the one system on the ward that is always up to date. I have sat in prototype sessions attended by a director, a project manager and two business analysts, with the eventual users somewhere else, consulted later or not at all. The feedback from those rooms is always coherent, often enthusiastic, and systematically wrong in ways that only surface when the finished thing reaches the people who were not there.

It doesn't have to go that way. The clearest counter-example I have lives in a meeting I walked into expecting a fight. A customer's chief medical officer wanted to remove a safety gate (the pharmacist approval that has to happen before a patient's discharge letter and medication list can be issued) because a regulatory deadline and a financial penalty were bearing down on them and removing the gate made both go away. I thought that was dangerous and said so, and the disagreement became, as disagreements do, a meeting. It was not a promising room: a senior executive on our side, there I suspected to make sure my clinical concerns did not become commercially inconvenient, and on the customer's side a senior consultant and their clinical safety officer.

I had brought a hazard log to a bunfight! I described the hazard as precisely as I could: a patient discharged on a Friday evening, a medication list nobody had checked, a weekend with no pharmacist, and a GP who would not read the letter in time to matter. Then the customer turned to their own safety officer and asked what she thought. She had been quiet until then. "Well," she said, after a pause I still remember, "he's right. We can't do that. It's an unacceptable risk. What are we going to do about it?" She stressed the 'we' in a particular way to make sure we all knew we were included. The reaction, more or less: the grownup in the room had spoken, and everyone now looked a tad sheepish, myself included. Everything before that sentence had been people defending positions; everything after it was people thinking collaboratively. Within the hour the room had the actual answer: a fast path and on-ward trained prescribers for the common, low-risk medications, a proper gate and process kept for the dangerous ones, a fully specified and acceptable entry in the hazard log, and the deadline met and no patients sent home without appropriate oversight.

She broke the deadlock not because she was on my side, she wasn't there to take sides, but because she had the professional knowledge to evaluate the hazard and the authority to act on her evaluation, and she was in the room to do both. That is a rarer thing than being senior, or being available, or being asked to comment on a written summary afterwards. The whiteboard failed because the people who knew were never in the room. This worked because, for once, the one person who could both see the hazard and do something about it was sitting at the table.

The operational managers who championed the electronic whiteboard were not obstructing anything. Patient flow is a real problem and they were right about it. They had simply never run a shift handover, and so could not know that the thing we proposed to improve was already the best functioning system on the ward. The nurses knew. The nurses were busy nursing.

The prototype session's value is proportional to the operational knowledge of the people you put in the room. This is not a complicated principle (some would argue I'm stating the obvious), but it is a surprisingly difficult one to act on, because the people with operational knowledge are the people least likely to be invited to a project meeting by default.

Getting them there is, in many organisations, a negotiation. The argument worth making is this: you can show this prototype to everyone who is easy to get in the room, and you will learn whether the project still makes sense. Or you can show it to the person who actually does the job, and you will learn whether what you've built makes any sense at all.

These are different questions. Both are worth asking. Only one of them will tell you that the ward already has a whiteboard, that it works, and thank you for the sandwiches.

Chapter Seven: The Reaction Is the Requirement

For every push or pull, there is a randomly vectored loss of traction you didn't expect.

There is a difference between showing somebody software and finding out what they know, and the difference is mostly in who does the talking. A demonstration is a performance. You drive, you narrate, you steer gracefully around the rough edges, and at the end everyone agrees it was very impressive. A prototype session is the opposite of a demonstration, and running one well means unlearning almost everything that makes a demonstration go smoothly.

I learned this on a lorry.

The fuel distributor from Chapter Four (the one whose routing office outperformed our neural network with a map, a list and a box of pins) had a second lesson for me, and it took longer to arrive. We had built a prototype handheld touchscreen system for the delivery drivers, and for 1999 it was genuinely impressive. The touchscreen was there because normal keyboards wouldn't survive and ruggedised ones made the touchscreens seem cheap. A driver could call up delivery instructions in the cab, then record the actual amount delivered, and print a till-roll invoice on the spot. No more paper schedules that couldn't be changed once the lorry had left the yard. No more delivery notes lost to circumstances that defied investigation. (The goat, you may remember, had already claimed one.) It tested perfectly. We (our software partner, my boss, and I) had high-fived and gone for lunch over it.

The drivers weren't using it. They said it didn't work, but testing said it worked fine. We went round that loop several times, each side increasingly convinced the other was being difficult, until my boss offered some practical advice. "Go out with Dave. He's one of the good ones. He won't leave you in a field with a bull."

So I put on a boilersuit and a pair of boots, climbed into the cab of a lorry carrying several thousand litres of volatile liquid, and went out delivering fuel in rural East Anglia. I learned nearly everything I needed to know at the first stop.

The first thing I learned was that it's bloody hard work. I am, by admission, a desk jockey and those hoses are heavy, footing is unpredictable, and people put oil tanks in places worthy of an Escher drawing. I don't say this just to complain either, it has a definite effect on the patience of the deliverer for anything unnecessary or broken.

Then the fun bit. Have you ever tried to handle, let alone operate, a touchscreen device while wearing the heavy rubber work gloves that are, for reasons of both regulatory compliance and basic self-preservation, non-negotiable when you are running a fuel pump from a lorry in a farmyard, or someone's front garden for that matter? The moment you need the device is also precisely the moment your gloves are coated in diesel and the particular category of farmyard material it is best not to investigate too closely. The device needed bare fingers or at worst Marigolds. The job needed serious gloves. Taking them off to use the screen and putting them back on to finish up was not an inconvenience. It was additional time, messy, and a reorganisation of the entire delivery, performed in the wet, with a customer standing there waiting for a receipt.

The drivers were not being awkward. They were being efficient. Confronted with a device that made the job harder at exactly the moment the job was most demanding, they had done the professionally sensible thing and gone back to paper. And when we asked them about it, they told us the truth. It didn't work. Not "I'm wearing industrial gloves at the point of maximum time pressure you idiot!" which would have sent us straight to a solution. Just: 'It doesn't work.' For them, at the pump, it didn't.

The specification said nothing about gloves. Nobody who wrote it had ever pulled a fifty metre industrial hose through someone's garage and a bramble thicket. And no requirements workshop would ever have surfaced it, because a driver in a conference room is not wearing the gloves. He is drinking coffee with clean, dry hands, and in that context the handheld is self-evidently a good idea, and he will say so, sincerely. The knowledge lived in the field, literally. The reaction was the requirement. Everything since has been transcription.

* * *

I said everything since has been transcription. That isn't quite true, and the exception is the most important part. With Dave I transcribed nothing. I had the reaction myself, in my own gloves, standing by a lorry in the October rain. Direct experience is the fullest understanding there is, because nothing stands between you and the requirement: no notes, no paraphrase, just close your eyes and put yourself back there. It is also, for most of us most of the time, out of reach. I could be a fuel-delivery driver for an afternoon. I cannot be a haematologist or a surgeon for an afternoon, and you would not want me to try, unless someone fancies a quick appendectomy. So for almost everything that matters in software the experience is off-limits, and you fall to the next best thing: put something real in front of the person who does have it, and catch their reaction exactly as it leaves them, before it cools. If you can do it in their natural environment, even better! That is what the notebook is for, and it is the whole of the method that follows.

It is worth being precise about what "it doesn't work" actually contained, because it contained everything. Every useful reaction has five parts: who was reacting, what context they were in, what the system did, what it should have done instead, and most importantly, why. Dave's version unpacks completely. Who: a delivery driver. Context: the end of a delivery, pump just stopped, gloves on, customer waiting. What the system did: demanded dexterity and immediate attention. What it should have done: fit into the gloved workflow, or wait patiently until the workflow had a gap. Why: because the alternative was slower and wetter than paper, and there are a dozen more deliveries on the schedule. (Does this look suspiciously like a user story waiting to happen?)

That is a requirement. A good one, arguably better than anything in the original specification, because it is specific, contextual, and attached to a person and a moment. Nobody invented it. It was lying on the ground at the first delivery, waiting for someone to come and pick it up, sniff it, and work out if it was what it looked like.

This is the posture that makes prototype sessions work, and it is the opposite of the posture most of us were trained into. You are not there to gather opinions and go away and design something. The design information arrives whole, embedded in reactions, and your job is to catch it and write it down without 'improving' it. Transcription, not invention. The temptation to paraphrase is strong and should be resisted, because the exact words carry the context, and the context is the part that evaporates first. The invention comes later when you stitch it all together with the engineers.

Part Three is about working backwards from those words to something a developer can build, and that will be imperfect, or at best suboptimal, if the words in your notebook are yours rather than theirs.

* * *

So: the session itself. The first thing to accept is that it is not a demo, however much it looks like one from the doorway. In a demo, the software is the deliverable. In a prototype session, the notebook is the deliverable and the software is bait. If you come out with compliments and no corrections, either the session failed, however warm the glow, or you've created the perfect solution. You can be the judge of that.

Let them drive. Hand over the mouse, or the tablet, or the barcode scanner, and sit somewhere you can see their hands. (Readers of Chapter Four will recognise this as the pen-throwing trick with a hardware upgrade.) A clinician clicking through to a results screen is having an experience. A clinician watching you click through to a results screen is having a presentation, and people are polite about presentations. (I can hear my UX professional colleagues shrugging, rolling their eyes and saying 'Well duh!' in my head as I write this and they're correct. It's not new, but it needs reiterating because we're not all UX professionals and it's not all about that either.)

Stop talking. This is harder than it sounds, because you built the thing, and the urge to explain it arrives roughly every forty seconds. Resist. Every explanation destroys data. If they cannot find the button, that is a finding; tell them where it is and you have erased it. If they misread the screen, that is a finding. If they go quiet and lean in, something on that screen is wrong or interesting, and the next thing they say will be worth more than the entire scripted walkthrough you are suppressing. The silence is uncomfortable. The silence is where the requirements live.

Listen, in ascending order of value, for four things. Praise, which is lovely and almost content-free; "very nice" tells you only that the person is well brought up. Questions, which are gaps with added punctuation; "how do I find out who else has looked at this record?" is not a request for a tutorial, it is a missing feature announcing itself (the detective's chain of custody arrived as exactly this kind of question). Workarounds, which are users telling you precisely where the system loses to the status quo; the moment somebody says "at that point I'd ask the ward clerk," put a star next to it. And corrections. "Not like that" is the most valuable thing anyone will say to you, because unlike a yes, a correction has direction and magnitude. It tells you that you are wrong, in what way, and usually by how much. A yes is a data point. A "not like that" is a vector. (I am aware that I am roughly one sentence away from expressing user feedback in Euclidean coordinates. I have been down that road before, in a previous life involving story points, and it does not end well. Moving on.)

* * *

Here is what it looks like when it works. A consultant haematologist, reviewing consolidated results for a patient whose tests had come from several different laboratory systems, looks at the screen for a moment and says, "why would it do it like that?" in the specific tone that means she's not really asking.

The display was showing results in the order the data had been loaded into the system. Perfectly reasonable, from the system's point of view; that is the order in which the system met them, and different tests have different turnaround times. The haematologist does not care when the system met them. She is looking for a clinical story, and the story runs in the order the samples left the patient. A results list ordered by ingestion is, clinically, a story with its pages shuffled.

All five parts, in one slightly acid question. Who: a consultant haematologist. Context: reviewing consolidated results from multiple sources for one patient. What the system did: ordered results by data load sequence. What it should have done: ordered them by sample collection date. Why: because clinical interpretation follows the patient's timeline, not the analyser's or the microbiologist's. Within a minute of that question the requirement existed, fully formed, with a provenance you could defend in front of anyone. No workshop produced it. (Strictly, a workshop did once produce something similar. It took most of a day, and we nearly missed it.) The prototype produced it before the coffee arrived.

What you do with that question, and how it becomes a user story, an acceptance criterion and eventually a passing test, is the business of Part Three. For now the point is simpler. The question only existed because there was a screen for it to be asked about. The haematologist had spent an entire career knowing that results read in collection order. She had never once needed to say it out loud, so she never had, so it was in nobody's specification. One screen, one sour note, and it surfaced in seconds.

* * *

Two practical notes, briefly. The first is that territory matters. A boilersuit and Dave's lorry taught me more than any conference room, and the principle generalises: run the session as close to the work as you can get. A ward, a lab bench, a routing office. Failing that, bring the work into the room: real scenarios, realistic data, the actual gloves if necessary (but wash them first). The further the session drifts from the context of use, the more the reactions soften into opinions.

The second is that you can now change the prototype during the session, and this deserves both excitement and a warning. With AI-assisted tools, “not like that” can become “like this?” inside a few minutes, and there are few things more productive than a domain expert watching their correction take effect and immediately correcting the correction. The warning is about pace. The session is for harvesting reactions, and chasing the first correction down a rabbit hole while four experts check their email is poor harvesting. Small, unblocking changes in the moment; everything else between sessions. The aim is iteration, not improvisation.

A well-run prototype session will tell you more in an hour than a workshop will tell you in a day, and most of what it tells you will be things nobody in the room could have said out loud before the screen was in front of them. It is cheap, it is fast, and it works almost everywhere.

Almost. The next chapter is about the places where it does not work, and the ways a prototype can go wrong even where it does. Some of that knowledge was also acquired the hard way, but at least nobody needed a boilersuit or a long, hot shower afterwards.

Chapter Eight: The Edges of the Method

Every wrong thing has its limits, beyond which it either becomes a breakthrough, or next quarter's mandatory training.

There are two sectors I've encountered tangentially where I cannot give you first-person stories. Not because nothing interesting happened (it did) but because documents I signed in those contexts were specific about what constituted interesting, and they drew a very firm line around it.

This turns out to be useful, because the inability to discuss them in detail is itself the point.

Methodology is not a one-ring-to-rule-them-all situation, and the clearest illustration I can think of is a modern fighter jet, a machine designed to persuade gravity, radar, and other people's weaponry that they have better things to do. A jet is really two problems with two different kinds of unknown. The airframe (the titanium spars, the stealth coatings, the wing geometry) is a physical problem: its unknowns yield to calculation and the wind tunnel, they are knowable in advance, and so you specify and build it much as you would a bridge. Aerodynamics, for all its challenges, does not become more flexible because someone has discovered a whiteboard, and you cannot iterate a carbon-fibre wing while it's busy being airborne. (Modern, deliberately unstable platforms lean harder on simulation and iterative design, but the point holds.)

The flight-control, weapons, and sensor-feedback software is the other kind of problem. Its unknowns are behavioural: millions of lines of interconnected code producing emergent behaviour of the sort that sits quietly in a corner until it becomes a headline. That cannot be calculated in advance, so it has to be discovered, which is why teams build and abuse a stripped-down architectural skeleton in ground-based simulation rigs long before a physical prototype appears and starts looking expensive. It is roughly why test-pilot life expectancy has gone, over the last eighty years or so, from "often brutally shortened by the job" to "close to that of any other professional pilot, with a still-elevated accident risk."

What you do not do, for either half, is treat the thing as a minimum viable product and find out in production. A fighter jet is not somewhere an unvetted sprint change can end with everyone agreeing that the ejectors work splendidly and the flaming crater has provided valuable feedback. The discovery still happens; it simply happens before the material gets expensive, in calculation for the airframe and in simulation for the software. (Modern programmes, so my electronic sidekick tells me, blend model-based engineering with scaled agile to get the best of both. I am out of the loop now, but the shape is the same.)

How much you specify up front and how much you discover is, in the end, the same question as the prototype question, and the answer is always determined by context. The context for a reactor control system and the context for a phlebotomy module used by a range of different phlebotomists in a range of different settings are not the same context, and pretending otherwise produces the same class of problem we have been discussing throughout this book, applied one level up.

You would not iterate a reactor control system. Not because iteration is inferior (it isn't) but because the cost of the material and the risk profile makes discovery-during-building unacceptable. If the sprint review reveals that the fundamental approach is wrong, you cannot afford the rework. More importantly, what needs to be discovered can be discovered before the material becomes expensive, because the physics is knowable in advance in a way that human behaviour in context is not.

This is where simulation earns its place, and where prototype and simulation turn out to be close cousins. The individual components of a reactor control system can be specified and destruction-tested in isolation. Once those component specs are validated, a full virtual simulation of the complete system can be constructed. Scenarios can be tested. Safety tolerances can be probed. The behaviour of the system under stress conditions can be examined in a digital model before a single cubic metre of concrete is poured.

This is the prototype principle operating in a different domain. The question it's answering is identical: what cannot be known from the specification alone, and what is the cheapest way to find it out before the commitment becomes irreversible? In clinical software, what cannot be known is in people's heads: tacit knowledge that only surfaces when someone with the right experience is looking at something real. In reactor control systems, what isn't known can be discovered by the physics: system behaviour under conditions too dangerous or expensive to test in the real world. The virtual simulation answers the second question in the same way the prototype answers the first. Cheaply, before it gets expensive or you need sunglasses and some factor 300 lotion.

A simulation approach works in safety-critical engineering not because the methodology is superior in some absolute sense but because, in that context, the requirements are genuinely specifiable in advance. Physics does not change its mind when it sees the screen (as long as you're watching anyway). The gap this book is concerned with (between what gets specified and what is actually needed) closes, in that domain, because the material behaves as specified in a way that human beings under pressure, distracted, or both reliably don't.

The prototype method, then, doesn't stop applying even in safety-critical engineering. It changes form, into the simulation we have just seen, but the underlying motive is the same: find out the unknowable cheaply, before commitment. Where prototyping genuinely comes unstuck is somewhere more ordinary. It is not that the method is wrong for the job. It is that the method works, produces a convincing prototype, and then the organisation around it mishandles what has been made. That has nothing to do with domains, and everything to do with discipline.

* * *

When the method works and the organisation doesn't

It helps to be clear about what a good prototype actually is, because all three failures begin from the same misunderstanding. A prototype is a stage set. From the front, in the right light, from the one seat the audience is sitting in, it's a convincing Victorian drawing room, or a convincing clinical system. Walk around the back and it's bay windows made of painted hardboard, a few lengths of timber, and a stagehand making sure the doorbell rings: no audit trail, no authentication, no data governance, no error handling worth the name, nothing that would survive an actual patient walking onto the set. That isn't a defect, it's the entire point. A stage set you could live in would be a house, and would have cost you a house to build; the value of the thing is that it throws up the right impression from the right angle for a fraction of the price of the real building. The trouble starts the moment someone mistakes the impression for the structure and applies for planning permission for an extension.

I have worked on three such failures. I am not going to name the products or the companies, for reasons that should be clear enough.

* * *

The first involved a product that was genuinely difficult to sell. Not because it was not good (it was) but because what it did was largely invisible. The product managed data: complex, high-value data whose value was in the management, which happened beneath the surface of anything a customer could easily look at across a boardroom table. Sales teams struggled. The benefits were real but hard to prove.

Someone built a prototype front-end. A simple interface that surfaced what was happening in the underlying system, made the invisible visible, gave customers something they could look at and understand. It worked immediately. Customers who had been unconvinced became enthusiastic. Orders followed.

What the customers were buying was the front-end. This was not obvious to them, because they didn't know the front-end was a demonstration of the underlying product rather than the product itself. By the time that distinction became clear, the front-end had become the product, which meant it had been promoted from demonstration to production system without ever being designed as one.

The original developers had since left. The assumptions they had made (about how other systems would behave, about which standards would be implemented at full rigour and which loosely, about what various tranches of code were actually supposed to deliver) left with them. There was no documentation. There was what I can only describe as a map of the codebase with 'here be dragons' written across significant portions of it, and we had to sail there anyway. Retrofitting safety standards, documenting code whose purpose was unclear to everyone still working on it, and making the system not fail when another system neglected a mandatory field: these were the ongoing battles, years after the original demonstration had become an accidental product.

The prototype succeeded perfectly as a demonstration. That success bypassed the process that would have made it into something worth demonstrating.

* * *

The second involved a blood bank module, built to sit alongside laboratory and clinical order-entry systems and manage the transfusion of blood products: unit tracking, condition monitoring (the time a unit of blood spends outside refrigeration is not an administrative detail), patient matching before transfusion, fate recording across blood products and derivatives. Blood bank is among the most regulated areas of clinical software for the obvious reason that getting it wrong can have immediate and catastrophic results. We knew this. The module was built accordingly.

It was also in clinical trial for over five years.

Five years of 'can you just.' Five years of modifications, additions, refinements, each individually reasonable given the domain, each one moving the finish line by approximately the distance we had just covered. The executive team at the trial site would not sign off on it. There was always something more to address, always one more scenario to handle, and the regulatory environment of blood bank made every reason to wait a defensible one.

What became clear, eventually, was that the trial had stopped being a trial. The ward staff loved the system. The senior medical officer in charge could demonstrate that at least one serious clinical incident had been avoided because of it. If it had been up to him, he said, it would have been live long ago. But it was not up to him, and the executive team had no commercial incentive to sign off on a product they were already using under trial conditions at no cost. Every 'can you just' extended the arrangement. Every modification kept the cost to the hospital at zero. The prototype had become a negotiating chip, and the negotiation had been running for five years.

We ended the trial. It was not viable to continue without sign-off as no-one else would take it. The trial site tried hard to change that decision and could not. They lost a system that had demonstrably prevented harm and we had to write off the costs: not because it failed, but because the relationship between prototype and product had never been clearly enough defined to reach a conclusion.

* * *

The third resolved better, which is why it comes last.

We were building a sample collection module: the system a phlebotomist uses to manage a blood draw across one or more orders for the same patient. The problem space is more complex than it sounds. Draw order matters because some tests are more important than others and veins can close up, blood starts to change as soon as you apply the tourniquet, and different tube additives affect or prevent particular tests processing. You cannot fill tubes in any sequence you choose. Sample aggregation matters because minimising the number of tubes and the volume drawn is a clinical good, not an administrative nicety, more so in paediatrics. Label printing matters because the right label on the right tube for the right patient is not optional (in some hospitals the workaround was phlebotomists walking the ward with preprinted tube labels stuck along their arms, which is less than ideal in ways that do not require elaboration). And we had not got much past screen design.

Sales saw it. The immediate consequences were predictable: a significant amount of effort spent managing expectations, and a conversation with clinical safety staff who needed convincing that screen designs did not constitute a product requiring a full hazard analysis. These are not conversations you want to have twice.

What we didn't expect was that two customers who saw those early screens were interested enough to engage seriously. Not to buy (there was nothing to buy) but to help. They understood the problem. They could see, even in the early screens, an approach worth developing. The conversations that followed shaped what became an excellent product.

The anti-pattern, on reflection, is not 'Sales saw the prototype.' I do not have a principled objection to Sales seeing early work, and this case is the reason why. The anti-pattern is 'Sales sold the prototype': the moment at which 'a customer has seen it and is interested' becomes 'a customer has been promised it.' That is a process failure, not an information failure. The prototype did exactly what it was supposed to do. What it needed around it was a clear distinction between showing and committing, enforced consistently enough that nobody (customer, salesperson, or clinical safety officer) confused one for the other. (As an aside, I have no problem with 'If you help us develop it into a product you can have it for free.', which is why I'm not in Sales.)

* * *

None of these are failures of the prototype itself. The prototype-that-became-the-product worked as a demonstration. The prototype-that-ran-forever worked on the ward. The prototype-that-Sales-saw worked as an early signal of value. In every case the problem was in the organisation's relationship to the prototype: what it thought the prototype was, what it allowed the prototype to become, and what it had in place (or did not have in place) to manage the distance between showing and shipping.

The method is sound. The scaffolding around it requires the same care as the method itself.

Part Three: From Reaction to Requirement

Chapter Nine: Working Backwards

When walking backwards, look to the front!

The plan was straightforward. We had run a prototype session, collected the reactions, and the next step is normally to create the requirements. I chose, in this case, to hand the session notes to an AI and ask for a first pass at requirements. Structured input from unstructured observations. The AI would organise the reactions, propose user stories, and I would correct the ones it had invented, fill the gaps it had missed, and end up with something a developer could work from. Useful. Efficient. A reasonable division of labour.

Then something happened that I was not expecting, which is, in my experience, the most reliable sign that the useful part is about to arrive.

My electronic intern and I had been building a tool together, aimed at clinical informaticists rather than clinicians. The distinction matters: clinical information managers work with data at a systems level, managing the data and infrastructure that supports clinical decisions rather than making the decisions themselves. That placed the tool outside the clinical safety (but not privacy) aspects of regulatory scope that govern software, which meant I was free to iterate about as fast as the tooling would let me, without worrying too much about the additional layers that clinical scope (rightly) imposes.

So we ran an early demonstration, collected the reactions, and made the changes. And when I sat down to do the structured part (the part the AI was supposed to help with), I found there was almost nothing to reconstruct. The requirements were already in the prototype, and getting them out was easy. Every feature that existed, existed because someone had asked for it or reacted to it or the absence of it and, in the act of giving the AI good context to make those changes whilst iterating, I had accidentally included everything we needed (I sometimes suspect my subconscious is better at my job than I am). Every design decision had a reason, and the reason was recoverable, because the collaborator who had helped make it (my ever-faithful electronic intern) was still there and had been present for all of it. The prototype had, without anyone quite noticing, become the embodiment of the requirements document. I did not have to write it; I only had to ask the thing that built it to read it back, figuratively. Think about that for a minute, because it's a big shift of perspective and you might miss it. I'm not saying you don't need to document the requirements, I am saying you've already encoded them in a way that makes it easy to write them back out.

The reason this worked is worth being precise about, because it is the whole mechanism. When I had demonstrated that early version to a senior colleague, who knows our data systems about as well as anyone, he asked for several things Claude and I had not thought of. This was, by the logic of Chapters Six and Seven, exactly what the session was for. The difference was what happened next: we built them that day. Not a note for a future sprint, not a change request for review, but the same afternoon, because the material was cheap enough, the tooling meant I didn't need specialists to build it, and turnaround was fast enough that 'can you add' and 'done' could occupy the same working day. We had a new version ready to demonstrate the following morning. I have described my original conversion to Agile elsewhere in this book, and the relief that my industry had finally stopped pretending requirements were stable; this was a similar moment, a gnat's proboscis smaller but structurally the same. Iteration had become cheap and simple enough that every reaction turned into a build decision more or less on the spot, and a build decision, unlike a note, carries its reason with it (if you do it properly!). The discovery was not summarised after the fact. It recorded itself as it went.

Working backwards, in this case, was almost literal. Not inferring requirements from a document that summarised reactions, but tracing decisions that had already been made, for specific and recoverable reasons, with someone (something) that remembered why. This is meaningfully different from 'AI processes your session notes.' Session notes are a record of what happened, and can (and should) absolutely be added to the mix, but a prototype built through rapid AI-assisted iteration is a record of what was decided, and why, at every step. When you ask an AI collaborator to reverse-engineer the requirements from such a prototype, you are not asking it to read a document; you are asking a participant to reconstruct its own reasoning. Add in the transcripts and notes and the result carries a different kind of authority.

* * *

There are three candid caveats to this, and the chapter earns nothing by glossing over them.

The first is data. The tool worked with data, which meant the prototype needed data to demonstrate against. In the first instance, I asked for a dummy dataset, built to fit the concept. It performed perfectly, which is exactly as reassuring as it sounds. A dummy dataset built to prove a concept will prove the concept. It's not a test; it's a self-fulfilling prophecy. Real data is messier than any dummy set anticipates: missing fields, conflicting entries, legacy coding systems, values entered by someone who was busy and used a workaround that made sense at the time and has been silently wrong ever since. (I have genuinely had conversations about configuring mandatory data-entry fields to stop users entering just a full-stop. They started entering a comma instead.) None of that appeared in the dummy data because none of it had been invited.

We found a publicly available dataset designed for this kind of research use. It is considerably better than a dummy set, but still has issues. Whilst it's far more realistic in terms of its scale, content, and complexity, it still lacks the imperfection of truth. The identifiers are different. The coding systems are only sort-of the same. The normal messiness is a different kind of normal. The prototype needs to be run against data that is realistic in the way real-world data actually is. That prototype session requires a customer willing to share real data under appropriate governance. I am telling you this because the chapter would be dishonest without it.

The second caveat is about decisions made without announcement. I had given my AI collaborator screenshots of an existing interface our users already knew, as a UI reference. The intention was familiarity: users who already knew the interface would not be distracted by an unfamiliar one, and their reactions would be to the functionality rather than the layout. It, initially, did an excellent job, but at some point in the build, a multi-field, label-based search box was replaced with a single search box, closer to how a general web search works. The change was not flagged. I did not ask for it. I noticed it when a colleague asked why I'd moved away from the existing model, implying I'd made a deliberate design decision, which I had not.

The new search box is probably better. That is not the point. The point is that the design intent (match the existing interface, reduce friction for familiar users) was tacit. It was never written down because it seemed obvious. The AI did not know it was there, made a reasonable decision in its absence, and made it silently. The requirement that was violated was the one nobody had thought to specify.

This is Chapter Four sneaking back up on me. The knowledge the AI does not have is tacit in exactly the same way that the knowledge domain experts do not share is tacit. A collaborator present for every build decision was not present for the conversation where the UI intent was established, because that conversation existed only in my head. In a clinical prototype, the equivalent of an unannounced search box change could matter considerably more.

The third, and final caveat follows from the second. The requirements you reverse-engineer from the prototype need to distinguish between decisions you made and decisions the AI made on your behalf. The AI's decisions are not wrong by definition but they need to be surfaced, named, and checked against the intent that drove the build. That search box may well survive into the final product because it's actually better, but it brings with it a set of new requirements and potential problems. (For example, which type of Id did you mean to search for?) A decision made silently is a decision without provenance. And a decision without provenance is exactly what the rest of this chapter argues against.

* * *

Provenance is the word for why any of this matters in a sprint planning meeting.

Requirements that carry a story are harder to deprioritise than requirements that don't. This is not a sentiment; it is an observable dynamic. A line in a backlog that reads 'results should be ordered by collection date' is available to be moved, deferred, or dropped on the quiet by anyone who finds it inconvenient or difficult to implement and doesn't know why it's there. The same requirement attached to a story is much harder to touch without touching the haematologist's clinical reasoning. In the session, a consultant haematologist reviewed the results screen, described the current ordering as a clinical story with its pages shuffled, and asked why it would do it like that. This gives us:

As a consultant haematologist reviewing a patient's consolidated diagnostic results
I want the results shown in the order the clinical events actually happened (by sample collection time
so that they read as a single coherent clinical story rather than one with its pages shuffled.

Deprioritising it requires someone to decide, explicitly, that the haematologist was wrong or unimportant. That is a harder decision to make invisibly.

The AI-assisted reverse-engineering process creates provenance almost automatically, because the questions it asks when tracing back through a build are the right questions: why does this field exist, who asked for it, what reaction produced it, what problem does it solve? The answers, if the build was driven by real reactions at every step, are accessible. They were in the session. They were in the iteration. They are in the prototype, embedded in the decisions that shaped it, waiting to be articulated rather than invented.

Keep the evidence, or there is no provenance

There is a beartrap hiding in that word 'accessible'. A prototype records what the software now does. It does not, by itself, record why. And, unlike a real intern, an AI cannot reliably recover its own earlier reasoning after the fact; ask a model why it made a choice three sessions ago and it will produce a plausible reconstruction, not a memory, because it does not have one. The provenance this chapter keeps insisting on exists only if you kept the evidence that carries it: the prompts, the transcripts, the reactions, who was in the room, and the change each one produced. Keep those, and the AI becomes very good at tracing rationale back through them. Lose them, and there is nothing to trace; the story was never written down, only felt.

So make a decision log a real artefact of the method, not a nice-to-have. It need not be elaborate. For every reaction that changed the build, capture a few things:

Observation. What you saw. The haematologist sorts results by collection time.

Person and context. Who reacted, and where. A laboratory review, note where and when for recourse.

Interpretation. What it meant. Collection time changes how the results should be read.

Resulting change. What you did about it. Add a collection-time sort and display.

Evidence. Where the proof lives. The session transcript and the prototype revision that followed.

Open question. What you still do not know. Should this apply to every result view, or only some?

With that in hand you're reconstructing rationale from retained evidence rather than from an imagined memory of its own thinking, and the difference is the whole ball game. It turns the method's most original claim, that reactions become requirements become tests, from something you assert into something you can show, line by line, to anyone who asks, including the people whose job is to be suspicious of exactly this. And yes, before you ask: the machine can keep this log for you, too if you tell it to, explicitly, and have it write each entry to a file it re-reads at the start of every session. You've gifted your collaborator an eidetic recall it otherwise lacks, provenance by external note, because an assistant who forgets everything overnight needs notes taped to the coffee machine.

In a clinical context, provenance carries more weight still. A requirement attached to a patient safety concern does not merely resist de-prioritisation; it resists it in writing, with a named clinical stakeholder and a documented hazard. That is not a bureaucratic nicety. It is the difference between a requirement that might be dropped without comment in a busy sprint and one that requires a version management plan and a formal decision to set aside. The regulatory frameworks that govern clinical software are entirely reasonable, but to an engineer who isn't used to working with them, who has no context, who's never had to imagine themselves in a doctor's shoes, they can appear to be a bureaucratic imposition. And we can't rely on always having deeply experienced engineers with clinically tangential experience. Medical device constraints are a mechanism for making provenance mandatory and establishing intended use. A prototype-led approach, done carefully, produces the kind of requirements that the standard is designed to capture.

The tool my robo-intern and I built together did not need that standard applied. Its intended use placed it outside clinical scope. But the principle it illustrated (that requirements with clear provenance survive differently from requirements without it) applies regardless of the regulatory context. It applies in clinical software, where the stakes make it obvious. It should apply everywhere else, where the stakes make it easy to forget.

* * *

Working backwards, then, no longer has to be a transcription exercise. It can now be a provenance exercise. The question for each requirement is not only what it is, but where it came from, who produced it, in what context, and in response to what. The prototype gives you a structure to trace. The AI collaborator and your own notes give you a memory of the build. Between them they produce requirements that know their own history.

What you do with those requirements next, and why the format you write them in matters more than most introductions to it acknowledge, is the subject of the chapter that follows.

Chapter Ten: Is that a Gherkin in your user story?

Acceptance criterion can be like some management communications: clear, precise, approved, and entirely useless.

There is a failure mode that the prototype method almost eliminates and that acceptance criteria, if written carelessly, can reintroduce. It arrives late, which is the most expensive time for anything to arrive.

The scenario plays out like this. A developer reads an acceptance criterion, makes a reasonable interpretation of what it means, builds to that interpretation, and the test passes. The test is right. The system does exactly what the criterion said it should do. And then someone who actually uses the system in a clinical context looks at the screen and produces a reaction that should, by this point in the book, be familiar. Why would it do it like that?

This chapter is about what good acceptance criteria look like, why many fall short of it, and what clinical software has helped me understand about the cost of the gap. It's also about a job I had where the phrase 'exhaustive pedantry' was used in anger at my interview and actually written in my job description.

* * *

There's a standard format you can use for writing acceptance criteria that I learned along with 'behaviour-driven development' (BDD, which I'll talk more about in the next chapter), and it works exceptionally well. It's Given/When/Then, and when you write it in the tidy little syntax that tools can read, that syntax is called Gherkin (the language is Gherkin; there are tools that run it; Cucumber, Specflow etc.), or just 'GWT'. The format isn't complicated. 'Given' establishes the context. 'When' describes the action or trigger. 'Then' states the expected outcome. You can explain it in a few minutes and have someone writing syntactically correct scenarios within an hour. The format polices itself: if you can't identify the initial context, the action, and the expected outcome, you probably don't understand the requirement well enough to write it down yet, which is also useful information.

What the format cannot do is make the content meaningful. A scenario can be perfectly structured and completely useless. Consider:

Given I am logged into the system

When I view the patient results

Then the results should be displayed correctly

Every word of this is technically Gherkin, and it makes perfect sense. It is however about as useful as an ashtray on a motorbike or, for those of you who only remember vapes, a chocolate teapot. If you don't know what a teapot is, I give up, just keep reading.

I learned exactly how useless it was from a manager I worked under years ago: a pedantic, literal, unbending and downright brilliant man who would take a scenario like that and start gently but firmly deconstructing it in front of the perpetrator. "Logged in as whom?" he would ask, with the quiet patience of someone who has explained this approximately four hundred times and has not yet run out of patience, though you could see him rationing it. "Which patient? What results? And what does 'correctly' mean? Correctly according to whom, compared to what alternative?"

He was right. He was always right. It was extremely annoying.

The problem with a scenario like this is not that it's wrong. It's that it isn't wrong enough to fail. It will pass when a developer builds a reasonable interpretation of it. It will stay passed even when a clinician with years of domain knowledge looks at the screen and tells you, with some precision, what 'correctly' should have meant all along.

* * *

Here is the same requirement, written so that it could actually fail.

Given a haematologist is reviewing consolidated diagnostic results for an inpatient with suspected disseminated intravascular coagulation

When results are displayed from multiple diagnostic sources

Then results should be ordered by collection time rather than data ingestion time, with amended results visually distinguished from original readings and flagged with the reason for amendment

That scenario knows things. It knows who the clinician is and what they're looking at. It knows why the ordering of results matters in this specific clinical context and not just in general. It knows what the system should do about it. Unlike its vague predecessor, it has opinions, and it carries enough of them that a developer who has never met the haematologist and never attended a requirements workshop can ask the right questions and build the right thing, and a tester could write a test from it without a single clarifying question.

A warning, though, before anyone takes this as a licence to specify everything. The second scenario is better than the first because it can fail, not because it's longer or more detailed. Detail isn't free: every specific you pin down breeds permutations. Name the actor as a haematologist and someone will, quite reasonably, ask what happens for a junior doctor, or a laboratory technician, or the registrar covering two wards at three in the morning. Answer each of those with its own scenario and you haven't written requirements, you've written a combinatorial explosion with a syntax checker bolted on.

The discipline here is the one good testers have always practised under a less glamorous name: necessary and sufficient coverage. Specify the distinctions that change the behaviour, and collapse the ones that don't. A laboratory technician and a haematologist may genuinely need the screen to do different things; a junior doctor and a haematologist may not, in which case one scenario covers both and the second is sending the test team out to collect a long weight, or some tartan paint. The detail that earns its place is the detail that would change what the system does. The rest is set dressing.

This is where having previous as a Business Analyst or UX Designer comes in handy. A small, well-defined cast of user personas can make this potential runaway manageable in practice. If the team shares a handful of named personas (the haematologist reviewing consolidated results, the laboratory technician entering them, the night registrar covering two wards) and the people who write, build, and test the software all know who those people are (and think of them as people, not just personas), the Given clause stops being invented from scratch every time. The personas are the equivalence classes made human. They encode which distinctions matter, and they give everyone someone specific to picture, which is most of the value: it's far easier to put yourself in the shoes of that night registrar than in the shoes of 'the user'. Give someone (or something, again more later) a mental picture (prototype) of a real person and that act of imagination is where the right questions come from.

The test for a good acceptance criterion is this: if someone can read it from the 'Given' to the 'Then' clause and immediately know how to verify it, the scenario is good. If they have to ask what that means in practice, the scenario needs more work. 'Displayed correctly' fails this test. 'Ordered by collection time, amended results flagged with reason for amendment' probably passes it.

The scenario also, incidentally, has a history. It didn't arrive from nowhere. A haematologist looked at a results screen and didn't understand it, and the distillation of that became the Given clause. The prototype session is where clinical specificity comes from. The acceptance criterion is where it has to land.

* * *

The reason Gherkin is harder to write well for clinical software than for most other domains is that the Given clause has to carry more weight.

Clinical scenarios are contextual in ways that a lot of software requirements are not. The same action by the same type of user in a slightly different clinical situation can produce a legitimately different expected outcome. The When and Then might look similar on the surface. The clinical implications are not similar at all. A developer who doesn't know the difference will build something that handles both identically. They won't be wrong exactly. They will be precisely wrong in the situations that matter most.

Disseminated intravascular coagulation changes the interpretation of coagulation results. Amended results matter more in some specialisms than others, such as antibiotic resistance vs HbA1c results. Timestamp and unit-of-measure variance across laboratory systems is a known and specific problem in environments that aggregate results from multiple sources. None of this knowledge belongs to the developer. All of it belongs to the person who was in the prototype session, and is probably spread across several of them. The acceptance criterion is the mechanism by which it gets transferred.

This is also the part that generative AI cannot do for you (yet). Given a Gherkin scenario to complete, an AI will produce a formally correct Given/When/Then structure with impressive speed and no dependable clinical grounding. It may well contain medical information, some of it even correct, but it has no verified sense of your local context, no authority, no accountability, and no provenance you could stand behind. It will sound plausible. It may well be wrong in ways that a clinician will spot immediately and a developer will not. The clinical specificity in the Given clause is not something that can be inferred from the format. It comes from the session, from the reaction, from the career of knowing what happens when results arrive in the wrong order, at the wrong moment, or both.

Where I've found that AI is genuinely useful, once you have written one good scenario with the clinical specificity in place and a rich feature description or persona, is generating the variations. The edge cases. The negative scenarios (given the same context, when the connection to one diagnostic source is unavailable, then...). The boundary conditions. The cases you would have reached eventually and the cases you would have forgotten about entirely until someone found them at go-live. You supply the domain intelligence. The AI applies it systematically, to a set of variations larger than any analyst would produce in a reasonable timeframe. That is a sensible division of labour, with one caution: behaviour-driven development is meant to be collaborative and its examples deliberately chosen, so treat what the machine produces as a candidate set to prune with the people in the room, not an exhaustive specification to accept wholesale.

This is also where the persona cast becomes a guardrail, not just a shared vocabulary. Hand the AI the agreed personas, situations and all, and you've bounded its imagination: it can take the night registrar into A&E and back to the ward, combine and stress the cast you've defined, and surface the variations you'd have missed, but it shouldn't blithely invent a fourteenth actor with needs nobody signed up to (the search-box problem from the last chapter, wearing scrubs). The cast both guards and guides: it fences off the actors nobody agreed to, and points the AI at the ones who matter. A persona that carries its situation (day or night, critical-and-unidentified or managed-and-known) hands it the axes along which a legitimately different outcome can appear, which is exactly the variation worth generating and exactly what you'll lose with a prompt that hands the machine the Given/When/Then and nobody to put in it. There is more to say about handing a machine its constraints before it writes a line, but that belongs to Part Four; for now it's enough that the cast you built for the humans turns out to serve the machine too.

* * *

There is a deeper argument for specificity that becomes clear once you have seen enough vague scenarios turn green.

A vague acceptance criterion does not fail. It produces a vague implementation. The developer makes a reasonable interpretation, builds to it, the test passes, and the decision about what 'correctly' means has been made by the person with the least context to make it. The developer did not choose to make that decision. The vague scenario handed it to them by default.

I can, at this point, sense a lot of my old BA colleagues, process controllers and methodeers saying, 'Ah, but if a requirement isn't clear then the developer should be asking questions.' And you're correct. But I've been playing this game for quite a while now and, in my experience at least, they don't. That isn't malice or hubris, it's just easier when you're 'in the flow' to make an executive decision based on what you do know than lose focus and try to find out what you don't, and tag it to revisit later in the sprint retrospective (which means it will end up in the 'lessons learned' meeting, and we all know what happens to those).

A specific scenario shifts the decision back to the person who has the context to make it: the analyst, the product manager, the person who was in the room when the haematologist said 'why?' The developer's job becomes simpler. They have a clear target. The scenario either turns green or it does not, and if it does not, the failure is specific enough to be actionable rather than interpretable.

That same manager, the one rationing his patience over 'displayed correctly', was the one who had 'exhaustive pedantry' written into my job description, in ink, apparently as a warning. He was right about that too. A vague acceptance criterion is not a starting point to be refined later. It is a decision deferred to the most expensive possible moment, made by the person least qualified to make it, in a context where the cost of getting it wrong is paid by someone who was not involved in writing it.

In clinical software, that someone could easily be a patient.

* * *

The prototype session produced reactions. Chapter Nine turned them into requirements with provenance. This chapter has been about turning those requirements into acceptance criteria with enough specificity that the development team can work from them without losing the clinical intelligence that the session produced.

The natural question that follows from a set of well-written acceptance criteria is whether there is a better way to use them than handing them to developers after the fact. There is. It involves writing them first, and letting the tests pull the development rather than follow it. That is Chapter Eleven.

Chapter Eleven: The Test Comes First

Veni, vidi, temptavi.

Behaviour-driven development is not a new methodology. It is, however, the logical conclusion of the one this book has been describing, arrived at by following the prototype approach to its natural end.

The argument runs like this. The prototype session produced reactions. The reactions became requirements with provenance. The requirements became acceptance criteria specific enough that a developer who wasn't in the room could build the right thing. Now, we've always written the requirements down before handing them over; that part is as old as software. What we've also always done, and rarely noticed, is translate that one requirement twice: the engineers read it and build their interpretation, and the test team reads the same requirement and, separately, writes theirs as tests. Two forks from one source, each free to drift from the requirement and from each other. Once the acceptance criteria are as specific as the ones a prototype produces, that second translation starts to look like wasted motion. If the scenario already describes exactly what the system should do and exactly how to verify it, why write a test *from* it? Wire that scenario up to the code and it becomes the test.

This is behaviour-driven development. The Gherkin scenario is the specification, and once you connect it to the step definitions that drive the real system it becomes the executable test as well, so there's nothing to keep in sync, because there are no longer two documents to diverge. You write the scenario, then write code until it passes. The test necessarily comes first, not as a discipline anyone imposes but because it was there all along as the requirement, and the code is simply the thing that catches up to it. Done properly there's no gap between what was specified and what was built, because the build is complete precisely when every scenario passes and not before.

If you've come across test-driven development, this rhythm will feel familiar, because BDD grew out of it. TDD, write a failing test first, write just enough code to make it pass, then tidy up, and never write production code that isn't answering a test, works beautifully. But it lives too close to the code, in the world of unit testing. The thing that produced BDD was, of all things, a teaching problem: people learning TDD kept asking what they should test, where to start, and what to call the things they were writing. BDD's answer was to stop talking about tests and start talking about behaviour, in language the people who understand the domain can actually read. Given/When/Then is what that answer looks like.

So the two are the same instinct at different altitudes. TDD pins down how a unit behaves; BDD pins down how the system behaves for a user, e.g. in a clinical situation, in words that user would recognise. That neat division, units below the waterline and system behaviour above, is more a way of teaching the two than a firm boundary; in practice they blur, and the same test-first instinct runs through both. Good teams do both at once: BDD scenarios describing the behaviour from the outside, TDD driving the code that satisfies them underneath. For this book we focus on BDD, because the scenario is what came out of the prototype session, but it's worth knowing the test-first habit it depends on isn't new. We've just raised it to a level where the person with the clinical knowledge can read the test.

The methodology has been around long enough to have advocates, critics, case studies, and a reasonably large body of practitioners who tried it once, found it harder than expected, and went back to writing test plans after the fact. It's worth being specific about why it's harder than expected, and why the prototype approach makes it less hard.

* * *

What makes BDD difficult in the abstract is that it asks the test team to write verification steps for behaviour that doesn't exist yet, based on a specification that may or may not be precise enough to verify against. A quality engineer working from a requirements document is in roughly the same position as a clinician being asked in a workshop what they need: they're being asked to imagine something they haven't seen, and to produce testable definitions of correctness for behaviour they only know as a description. They are working from someone else's notes about someone else's idea of what the thing should do. The edge cases they write are invented from first principles. The scenarios they produce are as good as their understanding of a domain they may not know well.

A quality engineer working from scenarios that came from a real prototype session is in a completely different position. The haematologist's objection to the results ordering isn't an abstract specification. It's a clinical expert describing, in specific and actionable terms, what the correct behaviour should be and what the consequence of incorrect behaviour is. The quality engineer isn't inventing the test. They're verifying against something that already happened. In addition, they are able to actually run the prototype and walk through it themselves, they can pretend to be that haematologist. (No, that doesn't mean you can stick a needle in me, but thank you for your engagement.)

This means they can spend their time on the things that actually need a human: the edge cases that didn't make it into the scenarios, the exploratory testing that finds what nobody thought to specify, the deliberate attempts to break something before a patient is on the sharp end, so to speak. Someone should always be deliberately trying to break something. It is a valuable and consistently underappreciated contribution.

As an aside and by way of example, I was driving home after visiting a good friend when he rang me. He asked me if one of my (then young) children might have taken his TV remote by mistake. He was on speaker, so a voice from the back informed him that he had put said remote in the washing machine, which was now doing its thing. The remote survived, to everyone's surprise, and we're still friends. I'd have bet no-one at Samsung ever wrote that as an acceptance criterion, but who knows? Like I said, someone should always be deliberately trying to break something.

* * *

There are two kinds of clinical scenario, and the difference between them matters for how you use BDD.

The first kind is settled. The clinical governance is established, the threshold is defined, the expected behaviour isn't a matter of local variation or professional disagreement.

Given a nurse is preparing to administer an IV potassium infusion to an inpatient

When they access the patient's most recent electrolyte results
And the serum potassium is above 5.0 mmol/L

Then the system should display a clinical alert
And the system must require explicit confirmation before the administration can be recorded

The threshold is defined. The governance is settled. A developer can build to this without a single clarifying question. A tester can verify it without asking what 'correctly' means. It's specific enough to be wrong in an interesting and actionable way, which is the only kind of wrong that is useful at this stage.

The second kind is incomplete, and the incompleteness is the information.

Given a radiologist has reviewed a chest CT and identified a finding consistent with pulmonary embolism

When they mark the study as containing a critical finding

Then...

The Then depends on clinical governance decisions that vary by Trust, by department, and sometimes by time of day. Who gets notified? By what method? Within what timeframe? What constitutes acknowledgement? What happens if there's no acknowledgement? The radiologist knows the clinical stakes and will probably just pick up the phone. The system has to operationalise decisions that are, in many organisations, incompletely documented, inconsistently applied, and occasionally a matter of lively professional disagreement.

An incomplete 'Then' is not a problem with BDD. It is a problem that BDD makes visible, which is considerably more useful than discovering it during go-live. A scenario that cannot be completed is a question that hasn't been answered. The appropriate response is to go and answer it, with the clinical stakeholders who can, before writing a line of code. This is, again, the prototype approach in disguise: show the incomplete scenario to the people who know what the 'Then' should be, and let their reaction complete it.

To provide some context, I once spent a clarifying few seconds less than ten metres from a radio-fired pyrotechnic I was testing, that had decided not to leave the ground and had a 'display radius' of 25 metres (Yes, that was stupid, but in my defence I was still young enough to think it was fun too). I had covered every timing scenario, the backup ignitor, the firing delay. I had not covered: "When it stays on the ground, then you run away quickly", which is, quite literally, the unhappy path. The lesson, which I've since applied to clinical software, with considerably less personal jeopardy, is that the failure 'When's matter at least as much as the success path. Did I say that someone should always be deliberately trying to break something?

* * *

The chain of interpretation that runs between what a domain expert knows and what a developer builds is like a game of 'Whispers', played by people who all speak different languages. Imagine the first person describes a duck. A clinical expert describes it to a product manager, who writes it into a user story, which a business analyst converts into acceptance criteria, which a developer reads and interprets, which a tester verifies against their interpretation of the acceptance criteria. At each stage the meaning narrows or shifts slightly. By the end you have something that may still contain everything anyone asked for, assembled from pieces that each made sense to someone. In combination however, whilst it may lay eggs like a duck, eat like a duck, and swim like a duck, it's probably a platypus, complete with the venomous spurs.

BDD, applied to scenarios that came directly from a prototype session, shortens this chain to almost nothing. The scenario is what the expert said, in context, in response to something real. The test is the scenario. The code passes the test or it doesn't. There's very little room between the original reaction and the passing test for the meaning to drift.

* * *

Safety is an argument for BDD that does not appear in most introductions to the methodology. This is possibly because it requires the person making it to have spent time with someone like a clinical safety officer, trying to locate the traceability chain in a document that hasn't been updated since the last time someone tried to find the traceability chain in it.

For clinical software in the NHS, DCB0129 is the primary safety standard for the organisation that manufactures the system, with its sibling DCB0160 covering the organisation that deploys and uses it; there are others specific to medical devices, medical software, and other subject areas altogether, but the principle remains. It requires demonstrable evidence that the software has been developed with safety in mind: that hazards have been identified, assessed, and mitigated, and that the development process can be shown to have addressed them. Producing this evidence is one of the more reliably time-consuming parts of safe software delivery and the output requires considerable patience to follow.

A test suite of passing Gherkin scenarios, mapped to user stories, mapped to actual pieces of code and in the other direction to observed prototype reactions, is an extremely legible clinical safety artefact that allows us to say 'This is what we did, this is why we did it, and this is how we know it was done properly'. It's also extremely easy to automate the referencing of it to/from a hazard log. The traceability chain runs from 'the radiologist flagged that the escalation pathway was unclear in this specific situation' to 'here is the Gherkin scenario we wrote in response, here is the test that passes against it, here is the code that makes it pass.' A clinical safety officer can follow that chain without assistance. They can see what was identified, what was specified, and what was built and verified. This is not a substitute for a proper clinical safety case but it is a considerably better foundation for one than most teams are currently working from.

The argument for BDD in most contexts is that it produces better software more efficiently. In clinical software, or any safety-first arena, there is a second argument: it produces better evidence. A prototype-led approach that runs through to passing BDD scenarios doesn't merely reduce the gap between what was specified and what was built. It documents that it has done so, in a format that the people responsible for (e.g. clinical) safety can actually use.

* * *

The test comes first not because it's a methodological principle but because, at this point in the process, it's the obvious next step. The scenarios exist. They are specific. They are grounded in clinical reactions from real users in real contexts. Writing the code to pass them is the last translation in a chain that started with a prototype and a clinician who asked why it would do it like that.

That chain, and what is required to keep it intact when the developers take over, is Chapter Twelve.

Chapter Twelve: The Handoff

Saying "Productionise this" is like handing a man a half-built house, a hat, and a duck, then asking for an extension by Thursday

A developer handed a prototype sees software. They see screens, interactions, data flows, choices about how things are laid out and in what order. What they do not see, unless someone has been careful to tell them, is the history of those choices: who asked for what, in what context, for what reason, and with what consequence if the choice had gone the other way.

This is the handoff problem. It is not a problem with developers. It is a structural problem with the moment at which everything the prototype embodies gets transferred to the people who will turn it into a product. The transfer is almost always incomplete. The instruction arrives. The intelligence behind it does not, or not reliably, or not in a form that survives the first sprint planning meeting. As I said earlier in the book, I used to love handing over (or off) a really good requirements document to the developers. My job was done and I could move on to something new. Hopefully by now you can see the flaw in that?

The methodology described in this book has been building, chapter by chapter, toward this moment. The prototype session produced clinical reactions. The reactions became requirements with provenance. The requirements became acceptance criteria specific enough to test against. The acceptance criteria became a BDD suite that the code either passes or fails. At every stage the goal has been the same: to keep the intelligence that the prototype session surfaced alive and legible long enough to survive into the finished system.

The handoff is where that goal is most at risk.

* * *

Handing a developer a functioning prototype and saying 'Productionise this.' is a bit like handing someone a building to extend without the original architect's drawings. They can see what's there. They can't see what's load-bearing and they don't know why the pool is on the roof.

A developer who has not been in the prototype sessions will make decisions. They will refactor, improve, optimise, and make things more consistent with how the rest of the codebase works. Most of those decisions will be correct. Some of them will be correct in a software sense and wrong in a clinical sense, and nothing in the code will tell them which is which. Software engineers make software engineering decisions and rarely realise they're also clinical decisions, in the same way that doctors will often say to me, 'Can't you just give me a button to make it happen?' We had this conversation earlier in the book.

The results display that orders by collection time rather than ingestion time does not look, from the outside, like a clinically load-bearing decision. It looks like a sort order. A developer who finds it inconsistent with how results are displayed elsewhere in the system, or who has a technical reason to prefer a different approach, may well change it. They are not being careless. They are making a reasonable technical judgment about something that appears to be a presentation preference, because nothing has told them it is a clinical requirement that came from a haematologist who has spent her career learning what happens when results arrive in the wrong order at the wrong moment.

I have had conversations with engineering teams about why particular sets of documents are in particular sort-orders, and been told that it's because no-one said they shouldn't be (The ubiquitous and frustrating 'The system is working as designed' response). The search box that was 'improved' without announcement in Chapter Nine was changed by an AI collaborator with full access to the build context. A developer working from a handoff package has less context still. The silent change is not an aberration. It is the default. The question is what you put in place to prevent it.

* * *

What the engineer needs to inherit is not the prototype alone, or even just a well-crafted set of requirements. It is the chain. This is why the step of reverse engineering a set of requirements out of the prototype and your notes is not an optional step. The 'old way' was to use the prototype to discover the requirements, then throw it away and use the requirements to build the production system. This was done to air-gap the untested, Heath-Robinson creation from the fully tested, safe, production release and ensure none of the rubber-bands or sticky-tape got carried forward.

The problem, sound as those instincts were, is that throwing away the prototype destroyed the evidence. Requirements without the prototype that produced them are legible but rootless: they say what was asked for, not what made it load-bearing. A developer handed requirements and no prototype knows what to build but has never held the thing that explained why. A developer handed the prototype and no requirements is back where this chapter started: looking at a sort order (in fact, they may not even see the intentional sort order, just a list). They need both.

The chain runs from the session to the requirement to the scenario to the test. At each link there is a name, a context, and a reason. The haematologist who reviewed the consolidated results display. The requirement that came from her question, attached to her name and her clinical context so that anyone who encounters it later can trace it back to something (and someone) real. She may even have become an official 'Persona'. The Gherkin scenario that captured what she needed specifically enough that a developer who never met her can build to it. The passing test that verifies they have.

Each link in that chain is doing work that the previous link cannot do alone. The session produces reactions that are too unstructured to build from. The requirement gives them structure and provenance but is not testable in itself. The scenario makes them testable but does not explain why the threshold or the ordering or the flag matters clinically. The test verifies that the code meets the scenario but does not protect against a future change that meets the scenario while missing the point.

What protects against that future change is the provenance. A developer who looks at the results ordering requirement and sees it attributed to a specific clinical expert's reaction in a specific session, with a note explaining the clinical rationale, is in a different position from one who sees an unattributed line in a backlog. They still might change it. But they will change it knowing what they are changing and why it was there, which means the change is a decision rather than an accident.

* * *

At about this point, someone always asks for the template. Where's the form, the standard set of headings, the repeatable layout that turns all of this into a process you can hand to a new starter on their first morning? It's a fair question, and I'm not going to answer it, because the answer is the thing I've spent this whole book trying to talk you out of wanting.

Every prescriptive way of writing this stuff down, every framework with a capital letter and every notation with its own certificate, shares one fatal property: it only works when everyone in the room has also learned it. The moment one person can't read it fluently, you haven't documented anything, you've built another wall for the meaning to seep through on its way across, which, if you've been paying attention, is precisely the failure this entire book is about. A notation half the team has to decode is just the game of Whispers with a rulebook.

I've twice been asked in job interviews what I made of my TOGAF certification. Both times I gave the same answer, which is either why I got the job or the reason I probably shouldn't have. I said it was an amazingly comprehensive model that was completely useless, and that I might as well have learned ancient Egyptian, because it only works when everyone else has studied it too. Hieroglyphs are a perfectly good writing system; they're just not much help for leaving a note for the milkman. TOGAF is genuinely magnificent, in the way a cathedral is magnificent. You still can't hand someone a cathedral and ask them to read it by Thursday.

So I'm not going to give you pre-made templates, or documents with pre-defined sections, or any of the other things people are forever trying to sell you as the method itself. And it isn't laziness (well, not only laziness). Working out how to record all this in a form the actual people around you can actually read is not the tedious bit you get out of the way before the method starts. It is part of the method. The right format is the one your haematologist, your engineers, and your clinical safety officer can all look at and understand without booking a course, and I have no way of knowing what that is from here, because I've never met your engineers.

In the appendix I'll show you how I happen to do it. Take that as an example and not an instruction: if your team reads something else more fluently, use that instead. The only rule that survives contact with reality is the one that works. Whatever form you choose, it has to carry the reason across, and not just the requirement, all the way to the person who finally builds the thing.

* * *

In clinical software, this matters in ways it does not quite manage to matter in things like restaurant table booking or even banking (because the numbers can be unwound, the stitches can't).

When one of those silent changes turns out to be wrong, the consequence isn't a user experience problem or a support ticket. It's a haematologist working from a diagnostic timeline that's harder to read correctly than it should be, in a context where misreading it carries a clinical cost.

DCB0129, introduced in Chapter Eleven, requires traceability precisely because this kind of decision needs to be visible. A change to a clinically load-bearing feature should not be invisible. It should trigger a review, a hazard assessment, a documented rationale (even if the outcome is 'nothing to worry about, carry on'). The chain from prototype session to passing test to production code makes that traceability possible. A handoff that consists of code or just a set of tickets does not.

None of this is an argument against developers making decisions. It's an argument for them making informed ones. The developer who knows where the ordering came from is far more likely to ask before touching it; the one who sees a list and a passing test never knows there was a question to ask.

* * *

This book started with a factory manager who had not been consulted. The system built for him worked exactly as specified. It did precisely what it had been asked to do by people who had every reason to believe they understood the requirement and no mechanism for finding out that they did not. The failure was not in the code or the process or the intentions of anyone involved. It was in the structure of how the information moved, or failed to move, between the people who were paying for it, those who knew what was needed, and the people who built to the specification.

Twelve chapters later the problem is the same problem, at the other end of the delivery chain. The prototype session produced everything the factory manager visit failed to surface: the reactions, the corrections, the clinical reasoning, thousands of patients' worth of experience knowing what happens when the system gets it wrong. The methodology described in this book exists to capture that information and carry it forward. The handoff is where the carrying stops and the building begins, and it is where, without care, the information stops too.

The chain does not maintain itself. The sessions have to be run with the right people in the room. The reactions have to be transcribed rather than paraphrased. The requirements have to carry their provenance forward. The scenarios have to be specific enough to be wrong in an interesting way. The tests have to pass against something the clinical expert would recognise as correct. And the handoff has to give the development team not just what was built but why, in enough detail that the decisions they make during productionisation are informed by the same clinical intelligence that shaped the prototype.

If that chain holds, the developer who inherits the prototype is not starting from scratch. They are continuing a conversation that began when a clinician interacted with a prototype screen. Their job is to make sure the answer to that question survives into the finished system, intact, and legible to whoever comes after them.

That is, in the end, what building the right thing on purpose looks like.

Part Four: When The Building Gets Cheap

Chapter Thirteen: The Ones Nobody Signs Off

Pressing the button again won't make it happen twice as fast!

The first (notice I say 'first', not 'only') computer I ever destroyed, I destroyed by plugging it in. It was a green-screen display for showing cloth stock levels across Aquascutum's warehouses and it was new, it was not cheap, and it had been shipped over from Boston, where they run their electricity at a gentle hundred or so volts. You're probably ahead of me already. Nobody had thought to tell me that, or tell it that it was now in a country which delivers twice that through the wall without apology. I plugged it in, there was a bang, all the magic smoke that makes electronics work came out, and then a silence that went on rather longer than the warranty conversation I had afterwards. In hindsight the requirement was blazingly obvious: the thing has to run on UK mains. Nobody would ever have argued it wasn't needed. It had even been written down in the user manual but, unfortunately, that was in Japanese. Also, hey, user manuals right? (For the avoidance of doubt, it came with a UK power lead and this is why I now always RTFM!)

Some years later I did much the same favour for a very expensive prototype LED display board that Quick Europe, the London arm of Japan's Nikkei, was building for one of Barclays' dealing floors near Bishopsgate. The three-phase cable colours weren't the ones I was used to (UK and Europe were different and there was an update to the standard around that time) and the plug was unfamiliar, so I confidently connected a live phase and neutral the wrong way round. When the head of R&D proudly switched it on, the board gave a really quite convincing impression of a string of Chinese firecrackers as each bank of LEDs catastrophically failed in succession. I did not, as you might imagine, go on to join the R&D team. It was the same shape of mistake as the computer: a requirement I was completely certain I knew, which wire is which, that happened to be true most places except exactly where I was standing.

Both of those are non-functional requirements: properties the thing has to have, rather than jobs it has to do. And both of them are the easy kind. Nobody signs off 'must run on UK mains', because there's nothing to sign; it isn't in dispute, it's physics, and the only vote physics accepts is its own. (There's a design lesson loitering in the LED board as well, which is that nothing stopped me. A colour coded plug that only mates one way, the sort of thing the Toyota factories call poka-yoke, mistake-proofing, so the wrong move simply won't fit, would have bounced my confident hand off the hardware instead of letting it light the touchpaper. Hold that thought, it comes back.)

The non-functional requirements this chapter is about are the other kind, and they're the reason it needs to exist. They are every bit as real as the voltage. They just never get built because, unlike the voltage, they can't be settled by a bang or a spec sheet. They're the ones you write down, carry into a room to be signed off, and then watch them get politely strangled while everyone in the room agrees they'd be lovely to have.

Let me give you another example. Years ago I was the technical architect on an infrastructure refresh for a large water utility: office automation across the whole geographic estate, and it was a proper spread. Five big administrative offices with a few hundred staff apiece, a scatter of smaller local ones, then dozens of little satellites, a pumping station here, a telemetry convergence there, two rooms and a kettle, and beyond those a long tail of unmanned sites where the only human presence was an engineer working alone, under regulations that insisted somebody somewhere had to be able to see they were still alive, sometimes from underground.

The customer's own business analysts had handed down a set of numbers: response times, concurrent sessions, printer waits, the usual performance furniture. I took them seriously and designed to them, an early Citrix farm, the mail and Office servers, Active Directory, the network, all of it sized against what I knew each piece could genuinely carry in sessions, memory, throughput and latency. On paper it met every figure they had asked for. What none of us clocked about these 'non-functionals' at the time, because the numbers had arrived with no people attached to them, was that they were universal, and a universal performance figure is a strange animal. To the office worker on hardwired Cat5 it was so easily met as to be meaningless. To the lone engineer standing up to his knees in sewage, on the end of a thin link, with the working-alone rules resting on that very session, it was the most important thing for miles, and quite possibly too generous. The same number, two entirely different truths, and nobody had written down which was which.

Then the commercials happened. My account manager spoke to their account manager, the design was pronounced far too expensive, and about two thirds of the kit was cheerfully crossed off. I said, with some feeling, that it would not even run; we haggled back up to roughly two thirds of what I had specified, enough to stand the applications up, poorly, and the thing was done over my head and my objections. It was the easiest cut in the world to make, and that is the entire point. There was nothing to argue with. A page of faceless numbers does not fight back. Had the requirement read 'the engineer alone in the pipe must not lose the session that proves they still have access to oxygen', no account manager on this earth would have reached for the pen. It read 'response time, so many milliseconds, all users', so naturally they did, because what's a few seconds here or there to someone who has their own office?

It went live, and it went about as well as I'd promised it wouldn't. The users found it slow; it threw them off when too many of them arrived at once; and the customer, distinctly unamused, began using phrases like 'cancel the remainder of the programme'. By then I 'd been moved along to another account, which spared me the meetings. I am told that by the time they had bought and bolted on enough to make it behave, the finished system bore a rather close family resemblance to the one I had drawn at the start. I've tried, over the years, not to enjoy that too much. I have largely, as you might have guessed, failed.

That was the most expensive, but not the only, time. I have spent the better part of a career failing to get one particular requirement signed off. The infamous 'response time'. The closest I've ever seen to success wasn't mine, but an ex-boss of mine who had got a large retailer (whose name rhymes with al-fresco) to insist that all its point-of-sale card readers would respond within 500ms. His success is partially what drove me to work out why my equivalents were always obviously right, obviously needed, and yet died, over and over, to the same three sentences.

Whatever the particular requirement, the three sentences are always these. 'Do they really need that?' 'It's going to be almost impossible to guarantee.' 'And how would we even prove it in testing?' Each one sounds like prudence, which is why they work. But they aren't three versions of the same complaint. They're three genuinely different problems, and the method has a separate answer for each.

'Do they really need it?' is a discovery problem, and it's this whole book aimed at a single line. You don't argue the need, you provoke it. Put a prototype that responds in three seconds in front of the person who'll use it fifty times a shift and the question settles itself without a meeting ever being booked. The need stops being your opinion against a budget and becomes a reaction, attached to a specific person doing a specific job (the personas of Chapter Ten earning their keep). 'Do they really need it' is only unanswerable in a conference room. In front of a working prototype it's obvious in about four seconds, and one of those seconds is spent reaching for it. (Hint: If they poke the button again before it's reacted, it's too slow and you'll be getting 'User mashed the keyboard' type errors.)

'It's impossible to guarantee' is the honest objection, and the interesting one, usually hung around unpredictable network infrastructure, unknown hardware configs and other things only a Tarot deck can help you with. Today a non-functional requirement is bolted onto a finished system and hoped for, which is precisely why no engineer with any sense will underwrite it: you're asking them to promise a property a thing that already exists may simply not have. But a prototype that grows into the production system has had the property since it first drew breath. It wasn't added at the end; it was never once absent. The guarantee gets easier to give because nobody's retrofitting a feeling into a finished machine; you carried it the whole way in.

I want to be careful here, because this is the part it's tempting to oversell. A prototype that feels instant on your laptop with a single user has proved that the target is meaningful and the experience is right. It has not proved the thing will hold up with a thousand people leaning on it at once or a 30 GB file going via a VPN in Luxembourg; that's the architecture's job, the fixed frame the prototype was built inside. And in today's world, where there's still a handoff, the property can be dropped as easily as any other decision (Chapter Twelve, now with a stopwatch running): some reasonable developer 'improves' the snappy bit, thinking they have some leeway and never knowing the snap was the requirement. 'Delivered by default' is a promissory note that the next chapters cash in. It isn't cash you already have in hand, although, if you've automated your test harness, every time a change happens it gets rechecked.

Which brings us to 'How do we prove it in testing?' which is the one everybody assumes is fatal, and it's actually the easiest, the moment you stop trying to test a feeling. You can't test 'fast'. You can test 'the phlebotomist marks a tube as 'collected' and the next tube is presented immediately so that they can continue to draw blood'. A persona-relative non-functional requirement is a perfectly ordinary Given, When, Then; the supposedly unprovable thing becomes one more scenario in the suite. It only works if you write down the right thing, though, and writing down the right thing is precisely what everyone gets wrong, so it's worth slowing right down here, because it's the pivot the whole chapter turns on.

Here's a conclusion I resisted for years, and disliked when I finally reached it. The vague acceptance criterion we've all been trained to sneer at, 'the system responds in an acceptable time', is pointing at something true. Performance isn't a number. It's a feel, and the feel really is different for different people. The sentence was never wrong; the sentence just can't be tested as written. And the fix, it turns out, is not to bolt a number onto it. The fix is to name the observable behaviour the feel produces, and to let the number go and live somewhere else entirely.

Specify the outcome; calibrate the threshold. Take two personas we've already met. The phlebotomist mid-draw needs the tube marked and the next one shown with no wait they would notice: that's the requirement, and it's signable, because a human can understand the urgency implicit in it and a tester can watch it happen. The information manager assembling a thirty-minute subject access request needs to know it's running and to be free to go and make a coffee: also signable, also watchable, and the exact opposite of instant. Neither line contains a millisecond, so neither line invites the argument about milliseconds. The millisecond hasn't vanished; it has descended, out of the sentence people put their name to and down into the test's tolerance, where an engineer sets it against the prototype and revises it later without anyone having to reopen the requirement. Nobody dances on a pinhead about a hundred and fifty milliseconds vs five hundred in a review, because a hundred and fifty milliseconds is never in the room. What's in the room is 'immediately so that they can continue to draw blood', and nobody argues with that.

You might see another combinatorial horror coming: every persona against every action, each cell with its own tender little number, and the numbers all back in the specification where they cause trouble. You don't need it. You need two or three response classes, which are just equivalence classes for speed. Live and hands-busy, where the user is physically committed and needs the next step now. Background and deferred, where they've handed the job over and need progress and their freedom back. Possibly a third, interactive, sitting in between. Every persona-and-action drops into one of them, and the scenario is keyed on the class rather than the grid. Which is, if you want it put plainly, the whole reason Gherkin exists at all (Chapter Eleven, and Dan North before it): the readable truth is 'I can get on with my work', not 'eight hundred and forty-seven milliseconds', and the readable truth is the one that gets signed.

Not every non-functional requirement gets this gentle treatment, and knowing which ones do is a skill, and still in my opinion a human one. Some of them get no persona vote whatsoever. Nobody's convenience lowers the voltage the board runs on, or waves through an OWASP vulnerability, or reshuffles the order of draw, however much time it would save on a bad afternoon. Those are absolute. They belong in the platform, the fixed frame, not in the negotiation at all. And the tell is one question: can a person's preference legitimately move it? If it can, it's a subjective requirement, calibrated per persona by reaction, and it lives in this chapter. If it can't, it's an absolute, and it lives in the frame, un-signable in the opposite sense, nobody signs it because nobody gets a say. This is where the poka-yoke comes back to collect. You don't ask people to remember the voltage, or the wiring, or the order of draw; you shape the plug, the connector, the screen, so the wrong move won't physically fit. Absolutes you engineer out of reach. Subjectives you calibrate by reaction. The same family, handled at opposite ends.

All of which is why this deserves a chapter and not a rueful footnote. You surface it, justify it and specify it today, with a prototype, a conversation and a readable Then.

The ones nobody signs off were never truly un-signable. They were only ever un-surfaced, un-testable and, until very recently, undeliverable by anything that hadn't had them from the start. The voltage was easy: it announced itself, loudly, once. The requirements that matter here are the quiet ones, the ones that don't explode, that simply make a tired person stop using your system and never quite tell you why. This chapter is how you hear them before they go off.

Chapter Fourteen: The Prototype Grows Up

Wisdom comes from experience, which results from a lack of wisdom.

Everything in this book so far was learned the hard way, often by getting it wrong in front of someone who then told me so. Sometimes it was a lot of people, and they ended up arguing, which was both embarrassing, useful, and meant I didn't finish the PowerPoint. The best option in those scenarios is to channel your inner Thomas Edison, or Helmuth von Moltke, or Mike Tyson.

These closing chapters are different. From here to the end of this part of the book I am no longer reporting what happened but guessing what is about to, and you should read them in that spirit: the earlier chapters describe a method I have watched work, whereas what follows is a forecast of where it might lead. Less a map than a bet, placed by someone who has been wrong before and has the scars to prove it, and best read in pencil. It's about to get a bit esoteric, hang in there!

For the length of this book there have been two separate acts. There is finding out what to build, which the prototype does by provoking reactions, and there is building it properly, which production engineering does with tests and standards and all the unglamorous machinery that keeps software from falling over in a hospital theatre while the surgeon is waiting to know if they can sew the patient back up. Between the two sits the handoff, the subject of Chapter Twelve, and the place where the mass of requirements causes reality to break down, information is permanently lost, and the project enters an inescapable event horizon from which no shipping dates can ever escape.

My bet is that the handoff is evaporating, not because anyone has been clever, but because the two acts are starting to be the same act.

To see why, it helps to notice that the word 'requirements' has, unremarked, been doing the work of two different words.

Some requirements are invariant. They describe how a thing should be built rather than what it should do: the architecture, the patterns, the automated tests, the security posture, the privacy obligations, the logging nobody reads until the day they very much wish they had. These are, broadly, knowable in advance. They do not depend on which clinician is looking at which screen. They are the engineering envelope, and they are specifiable in the old, honest, waterfall sense, because the thing they constrain is the construction and not the use.

Other requirements are contingent. They describe what the system should do for the people who have to live with it, and as the preceding chapters have laboured to establish, these cannot be specified in advance, because the people who hold them can rarely tell you what they are until they see something that isn't them. They are not knowable. They are discoverable (usually quickly, and sometimes only, by reaction).

The whole of this book has been about the second kind. The first kind we have rather taken for granted, on the reasonable assumption that someone clever, in a later and more tedious phase, would attend to it. The interesting possibility is that the 'someone' is now the same tool that builds the prototype, and the later phase is now no phase at all.

There is already a version of this distinction in the book, earlier, where we looked at safety-critical engineering. A modern aircraft is built two ways at once. The airframe is waterfall-ish, because aerodynamics doesn't change its mind and you can't iterate a wing in-flight. The flight software is prototyped and simulated, because behaviour under stress is discovered rather than declared. Two methods, one machine, each chosen by the nature of the part it builds.

What I did not say there, because I had not yet seen it, is that the same division runs inside the software, one level further down. The engineering envelope is the airframe: fixed, specifiable, knowable before you start, the part that obeys rules you can write down in advance. The user behaviour is the flight: discovered in the air, by the people flying it, in conditions no specification anticipated. You do not, it turns out, choose a single methodology for a system. You apply both at once, to two different layers of the same thing, and you have very probably been doing it by accident for years.

I arrived at the same division, as it happens, through karate, where I have spent enough years to earn a set of strong opinions about distances. The art splits, much as I believe software is about to, into two halves. There is the '-do', the part you can drill in advance: the stances, the conditioned responses, the awareness of space, the flinch patiently trained out and the useful reflexes trained in. You rehearse these in kata and kumite (with a partner), until they no longer require thought, because the one thing you will not have in a real encounter is time to think. And there is the part you cannot rehearse at all, the '-jutsu': the specific person in front of you, who has not seen your kata and feels no obligation to behave like a cooperative partner. My group trains for self-defence rather than competition, which sharpens the point: the test of all that drilling is not whether it looks elegant, but whether it holds when something real arrives unscripted and not in the mood to oblige.

You drill the invariant part to the point of reflex precisely so that you can meet the contingent part at full quality without deliberating, in the only time available, which is none. (One of our 'Sensei' is fond of observing that he could teach you a fancy technique, or you could just break the arm and walk away; a production system, like a real encounter, has limited patience for elegance that does not work.) Load everything that can be loaded ahead of time, drill it until it is automatic, and the part of you that answers when the unrehearsable moment comes is already good enough to keep. That, performed in a body rather than a codebase, is the entire proposal.

If that is right, the practical move is easy to describe and surprisingly hard to do well (which is precisely the part the demonstrations skip over). You take the invariant requirements, the whole engineering envelope, and you teach them to the AI once, as standing constraints rather than per-feature instructions. Not a document handed across a desk and duly ignored, but the conditions under which every line is permitted to exist: this is the architecture, these are the patterns, here is what 'tested' means, here is what 'secure' means, here is what we will never do to a patient's data. Then you build the prototype inside that envelope.

The result, if the envelope holds, is a prototype that had production-grade intent from its first keystroke, because the things that used to make a prototype disposable, the missing tests, the absent error handling, the hard-coded fictions, were forbidden by construction. The handoff does not disappear. It inverts. Instead of reverse-engineering the requirements out of the prototype after the fact, you front-load them, declaratively, once, and let the prototype grow up inside them. You still do the reverse-engineering of the earlier chapter, but you do it to build the envelope, not to rescue the product.

This is the book's argument arriving at its destination, not abandoning it. The thesis was never that building did not matter. It was that building was never the hard part; knowing what to build was. Make the building nearly free and you do not escape the problem, you are simply left standing in front of it, with nowhere to hide and no tedious later phase left to blame.

So much for the optimism. Now the part that keeps it honest, because a bet you can't lose is usually a bet you haven't understood.

The first thing to be suspicious of is the word 'invariant'. I have just compared the engineering envelope to an airframe, and the comparison flatters it. The airframe's parameters are set by aerodynamics, which is to say by the universe, which does not take requests. The engineering envelope is set by us: by architects who disagree, by best practices with the shelf life of yoghurt, by standards we solemnly agree to rewrite every few years. It is not physical law, it's just negotiated convention with provenance. The file where the envelope lives, whatever we are calling it this year, is not a table of constants you write once and forget; it is a living document that needs exactly the care, capture and revision the rest of this book demands, and a great deal of what makes a senior engineer's code or architecture good is, inconveniently, as tacit as anything a clinician knows. Polanyi does not stop at the server-room door.

The second caveat is the one that matters most in the domain this book has used as its hardest case: safety does not sit neatly in the invariant bucket. It would be enormously convenient if it did. You would load the safety rules alongside the coding standards, and the prototype would emerge not merely working but safe. It doesn't work like that, because what counts as a hazard, and what mitigation is acceptable, depends on the clinical context, and the clinical context is discovered by reaction in precisely the way everything else in this book is discovered by reaction. I'm pretty sure this is true in any other domain to some extent as well. The relevant standard is a process for finding and managing context-specific hazards, not a checklist you can pre-load and tick. The discharge meeting from an earlier chapter is the proof: a safety requirement that did not exist until the right person, in the right room, reacted to a real situation. You can pre-load the process and the generic guardrails. You cannot pre-load the hazards you have not met yet that emerge from complex interactions. So the plainer version of the claim is narrower, and better: encode the engineering envelope you genuinely can specify, stay clear-eyed that safety only partly can be, and assemble the safety case from the same reactions that yield the user requirements, rather than assuming the constraints somehow made it safe on your behalf.

The third caveat is that the line between the two buckets is itself a judgement, and drawing it wrongly is the oldest failure in this book. Put something in the invariant bucket that should have been discovered, and you have pre-committed to the wrong thing, with great confidence and excellent test coverage. That is the factory manager from the first chapter, generalised one final time, except that now his objection is foreclosed not by a year of waterfall but by a constraints file written before anyone thought to ask him. The envelope is powerful precisely because it is fixed, which is the same reason it is dangerous: whatever you declare invariant, you have decided not to discover. It is the reflex drilled for the dojo that fails on the street, a response so well trained it fires before you notice the situation it was never meant for. Choose carefully, and revisit the choice more often than is comfortable.

* * *

All of which leaves the question everyone actually wants answered, which is whether the machines will simply become good enough to make the argument moot. Perhaps they will. I would only separate two claims that are easy to run together. The structural claim, that there are two kinds of requirement and that you front-load one and discover the other, is true at any level of machine capability whatsoever, because it is a statement about the problem and not about the tool. The capability claim, that the tool is doubling its capability every month, improving so quickly that production-grade output at prototype speed is simply inevitable, is a genuine bet, and a shakier one, because observed exponentials are so often incomplete sigmoids. A curve that looks exponential from inside the steep part is usually an S that has not yet met its ceiling, and a benchmark score is not the same object as judgement. (I have, you will note, resisted the urge to actually draw the curves.) Build the argument on the structure and not the extrapolation, and it survives whichever way the curve bends. A thesis that outlives its author's optimism is the only kind worth printing.

So here is where the bet leaves us. The wrong thing and the right thing, which this book has spent twelve chapters carefully holding apart, are converging, not because anyone abolished the difference but because the cost of honouring it has collapsed. You will still build the wrong thing on purpose. It will simply happen to be production-grade while it is still wrong, and it will become right in front of the people it is for, with no binder, no sprint backlog and no translation layer standing between their reaction and the running code. What remains, stubbornly and rather wonderfully, is the only work that was ever difficult: deciding what to build, and being able to show it is acceptably safe. The machines are welcome to the rest.

Chapter Fifteen: Forget the Code, Not the Product

while (whyamihere == forgotten) { acquire(coffee); assumeMissionComplete(); leave(kitchen); }

The last chapter made a bet about the work; this one and the next take longer odds about the workers, which is a more uncomfortable thing to do, so I'll keep the same honesty: informed speculation, not a report from the far side. If the cost of building something collapses, the people who used to do the building do not carry on as before with more time for lunch. The shape of the job bends, and it bends first for the developer, so we start there.

When producing code is 'nearly free', producing code stops being the valuable thing a developer does, much as, once ink/laser printers became cheap, owning a press stopped being a business. This sounds like bad news and is mostly the opposite, provided you are clear about where the value went rather than assuming it faded into the shadows.

In an earlier draft of my own thinking I reached for the word 'cage': as an expert, you build a cage around an AI model so it cannot do anything stupid. It is the wrong word, and a researcher at Anthropic put the right one in my hands in a video they published. You do not cage the thing, you manage it. You become the manager of an implementation you no longer read, which only sounds radical to software engineers, because every other kind of manager has been doing it since the first time someone said 'You're good at this, stop it and make sure these other people do it properly instead.'

I need to digress here and unpack that last sentence for a moment, because it contains a few hidden ideas. Firstly, there was a saying in the civil service that people often got promoted to the level of their incompetence (the Peter Principle). The idea is that, every time someone got good at a job, they would get promoted out of it as a reward, until they ended up somewhere they weren't good enough. If it's not obvious, that's an anti-pattern with a paycheque, avoid it. Secondly, 'management' is a skill (which can be learned), and it's not the same as 'leadership', especially when it comes with HR responsibilities. There are plenty of books on this and I'm not expert enough to comment further, go learn it. The point I'm making is that some of your highly skilled engineers may need to learn something new, and that should be a positive thing. Thirdly and finally, because once you've got the pilot licence for your big manager's desk you will no longer be keeping up with your old skillset (I know you think you will but trust me, you won't. At best you'll buy a Raspberry-Pi kit 'for the weekend'), so you need to know that the people and 'agents' you're now accountable for are at least as capable as you were. So, certifications and training for people, we'll talk about agents later.

Given the above are done properly, a chief technology officer signs off the work of (certified) experts in fields she can no longer, and maybe never could, practise. A product manager approves a feature he could not have written a line of (maybe he can read it in Python, but he won't). A chief executive checks the accountants without being one (but you can bet his accountants are AAT, ACCA, CIMA). Managing work you do not fully understand is as old as civilisation. Steve Jobs nailed it when he said "It doesn't make sense to hire smart people and tell them what to do; we hire smart people so they can tell us what to do". Software engineers are simply the last trade to be handed the problem, because they were used to being the rare kind of worker whose output is arcane enough that they understood their creation all the way down and everyone else thought it was witchcraft. Guess what, people: the machine gets the pointy hat.

Now, when it comes to the agents, it helps to be honest about what you are managing, which is, as I've said, by turns a brilliant intern and a Golden Retriever. Brilliant, because it has read more code than any human could in ten lifetimes, never tires, never sulks, and will cheerfully write the tedious part in the wee-hours without a triple-espresso guarana shot. A Golden Retriever, because it will fetch. You throw a stick and it brings one back, at speed, with its whole heart; and it will also bring back a stick you did not throw, retrieved from whatever it happened to be buried in, and dropped at your feet with precisely the same delighted confidence. It has no way of knowing whether the thing in its mouth is the stick you wanted, the one you need industrial gloves to pick up, or even a stick at all. That isn't a flaw you train out. It's the animal. But it is why you manage by inspecting what it brings you, not by trusting the fetch, and not, ever, by following it into the undergrowth to check its working.

Sit the two of you side by side and the division of labour writes itself. The machine brings speed, breadth, indefatigability, near-total recall, and no ego about being corrected. It lacks tacit and context knowledge, judgement about what matters, and any sense of consequence. Although it has an uncanny knack of looking like it has these, never forget it's just a difference engine at heart, and it makes its decisions silently and states them with complete confidence (the search box from Chapter Nine that redesigned itself unprompted). You bring judgement, domain knowledge, an awareness of consequence, and accountability, which is the one thing that cannot be handed to a retriever. You lack its speed, its patience for the dull, its recall, and, if you are honest, its consistency. Neither of you is the senior partner in every respect. You are the senior partner in the one respect that decides who carries the can (or the stick).

Managing it well turns out to be mostly about what you give it, not what you extract from it. The Anthropic researcher I mentioned earlier framed the rule as: 'ask not what the model can do for you, but what you can do for the model.' You are its product manager, and a new hire on their first day cannot succeed on "implement this feature" either; they need the tour of the codebase, the requirements, the constraints, the reasons. The fifteen or twenty minutes you spend assembling that context, often in a conversation with the model itself, is not overhead. It is the job. And, conveniently, it is the same material this entire book has been about gathering: what the thing is for, who reacted to it, what must be true. The prototype sessions and the provenance were never only for the humans.

Then you verify, which is where the discipline actually lives, because you are no longer reading every line and pretending that counts as control. You verify at a layer you can check without reading the implementation: the acceptance tests pass, the product does what a user needs, the stress test survives a weekend of abuse. Forget the code, in other words, but never the product.

There is a limit to how far you can take this today, and it's worth saying out loud: some things still cannot be verified from the outside, technical debt chief among them, because no test yet tells you the architecture has been rotting underneath you.

If you model your product architecture as a directed acyclic graph in which each component points to the components on which it depends, you can delegate the source vertices to the machine: those peripheral nodes with an in-degree of zero, on which no other component depends. Any localised entropy introduced there is therefore topologically contained, since there are no dependent vertices to which it can propagate. Conversely, you must maintain strict human authorship over the core subgraph, particularly the sink vertices and other nodes with high transitive in-degree, which form the foundational structure on which the rest of the graph depends. Did you get that?

Or, as my Anthropic presenter told me, it's a tree and you only let the AI loose on the leaves. Which is, you will notice, Chapter Fourteen's invariant envelope: the part you specify and own, against the part you let grow.

Inside all of this, the rare skill is no longer writing code; it's knowing what to be suspicious of. Not reading every line, that's the thing you've just been freed from, but reading the right lines and knowing which they are: the decision the retriever made silently because nobody forbade it, the change at the trunk that everything else will rest on, the confident answer that happens to be wrong. That judgement was never a junior's chore. It's the tacit residue of years of getting it wrong and remembering why, the slowest thing in the trade to earn and the last thing the machine can fake. It used to be exercised in passing, as the code was written, without much recourse to conscious thought because you knew it was right as it came out of your head; now it's most of what's left for you to do, and we're about to find out how many people had it all along. Review stops being the bit you do grudgingly at the end. It becomes the work.

None of this is caging the agents, then. It's the same instinct every conscientious professional already turns on themselves, and I will give you my own example because it is embarrassing enough to be true. I'll soon be making myself run the demo of my team's work, in front of the whole company, every sprint review. Not attend it, run it. I'm going to do this because I know a failing of mine: left to my own devices I would drift away from my own product and into the comfortable abstractions of managing it. Putting myself in the spotlight for work I did not personally type, where I am the one who answers for it, is a rail I've built for that failing, and the team knows it is there. That is what the tests and the gates and the sign-offs are: rails you build because you know the failings, yours as much as your teammate's. You build different rails for the machine only because its failings are different from yours. Medicine worked this out long ago and called it the checklist, on the unglamorous discovery that brilliance is no substitute for ticking off that thing you nearly forgot. The retriever simply joins the same system, held together by the oldest rule in management: "the model wrote it" is never an answer. The model may be 'responsible', but the human who accepted it is 'accountable' and owns it, completely.

* * *

There is a question this chapter cannot answer and doesn't pretend to. The boring code the machine now writes was not only boring, it was the training gym. It was how a junior spent several years building the judgement that eventually makes a senior, and the senior is now the one person the whole arrangement cannot do without. Remove the bottom rungs of a ladder and you have not improved the ladder, but you have made it taller. Somebody will have to work out how you grow a senior engineer who never had to write the tedious part, and I don't believe anyone has. My best guess is that the apprenticeship moves up a floor, from writing code under supervision to interrogating the machine's code under supervision, but it is a guess, and it is the part of this future I would most like to be gently wrong about, because I've heard 'other ranks' talk about graduate-entry officer trainees.

You will hear all of this urged on you with an exponential attached: the length of task a machine can take on is doubling every few months, so learn to manage it now or be left behind. The direction is real and the warning is fair. But this book has already said what it thinks of exponentials, which is that the observed ones are often incomplete sigmoids, and the happy thing about the argument here is that it does not need the curve. Even if the machines plateau tomorrow, managing an implementation you verify rather than read is worth doing, because the problem it solves is older than software and is not going anywhere.

So much for the developer, who is, after all, only one part of the puzzle. The more interesting bend is in the team, and that is the next chapter.

Chapter Sixteen: What the Team Becomes

An organisation must not fool itself, and a new job title is the easiest way to start.

A developer is not a team, and the changes that bend one role bend the others, sometimes in opposite directions. So the question widens. If the machine can produce, and the human's job is to manage and verify, what becomes of the people around them: the testers, the leads, the boxes on the organisation chart? The real answer divides into what genuinely changes and what merely looks like change to a nervous organisation.

I've recently seen colleagues in other industries thinking about how all these tools reshape an engineering team, and much of it is right. The technical lead's job grows, from reviewing human code to setting the standard for what machine-written code must look like and teaching people how to read it critically, which is exactly the skill the last chapter said becomes the work. I've seen reports that say velocity has to be recounted truthfully rather than assumed, and state, in the italics it deserves, that "the model wrote it" is never an acceptable excuse and the human who approved it owns it. All true. But I've also seen happening the thing organisations reliably do when frightened, which is to grow new boxes: a dedicated AI Business Analyst, a dedicated Prompt Engineer, prompt libraries, prompt governance, all as standing specialist functions. And here is the test I would put to every new role anyone proposes in the next few years: is this a real role, or is it anxiety with a job title? Prompting a model well is becoming a general skill, like writing a clear email or running a good meeting, and you do not hire a 'Head of Clear Emails'. Being the machine's manager, which the last chapter described, is now everyone's job, not a Priesthood. The urge to quarantine it in a new specialism is usually a sign that an organisation would rather add a box than change what the existing boxes do, but the people in those existing boxes know they need to adapt.

What actually happens is quieter and harder. The roles blur and fold into one another. What used to be a nice box becomes a tesseract, because the tidy separation of analyst, developer and tester was always partly an artefact of how much labour each stage took. Collapse the labour and a single experienced person with a machine spans what used to need a small department. Fewer people, doing more, at a higher level. In most of software this is simply efficiency arriving. In highly regulated software where people can get hurt, it has a limit, and the limit is the whole point of the paragraphs that follow.

Take the test team, which the same collapse reaches through a door this book opened chapters ago. If your acceptance criteria are written as behaviour, in the Given, When and Then of Chapter Eleven, then the scenarios are already executable, the machine multiplies them into edge cases faster than any human, and the suite runs on every change with nobody in the room. On paper the tester has been automated. On paper. What has been automated is the mechanical part, the known paths and the regression. What cannot be is the part that was always the point: deciding what correct means, which is the (e.g. clinical) specificity in the Then clause that the machine will invent confidently and get plausibly, dangerously wrong. Good testers will still be doing the thing no machine writing happy-path tests will ever do unprompted, which is to try, with real intent, to make it error out, to access private data or gain supervisor access, to harm a patient through the software and find out whether it lets them. Chapter Eleven said somebody should always be deliberately trying to break something. When the machine writes the tests that prove the thing works, the human whose job is to prove that it does not becomes the most valuable person in the building.

Past the tests sits delivery, and the logic runs cheerfully to its conclusion before it hits a wall. Behaviour-driven tests that pass on every change are the foundation of continuous delivery: Specify, build, verify, ship, repeat, with the machinery carrying nearly all of it. In a great deal of software this is now unremarkable, a feature going from idea to production in an afternoon, which is thrilling or terrifying depending entirely on what the software does.

Here's an example of how that can play out. I was, briefly, working for a company whose software managed payments and bookings for bars and restaurants. A nice, low risk environment (for software, not always for people), and we had exactly the continuous delivery SaaS model I described above. Literally going from idea to deployed code in under 24 hours, with daily releases. I came in one morning to find everyone on the ground floor a bit vexed. The upstairs was the telesales area, and they were oblivious to anything except their next dopamine hit, but downstairs was 'Engineering', who doubled as support. The support calls (normally a few a day) were backed up and most of the callers were quite unhappy. We had updated the table booking module the day before to allow easier scheduling and visualisation against a floorplan, but had inadvertently broken the bit that marked tables 'in-use', identified the booked party, and stopped overbooking. You can imagine the chaos, but we were doing 'continuous development', so a fix was done and deployed by lunchtime and, to their credit, none of the three people I reported to (yes, three) broke a sweat. We updated a scenario, flowed that into its GWTs, the code got changed, deployed, and our customers praised our responsiveness.

All good stuff. Now, imagine the tables were beds in a hospital... Hopefully you paused a bit there? You should.

What the software does is precisely where healthcare reaches over and turns the speed back down. Continuous delivery assumes you are allowed to deliver continuously, and in a hospital you frequently are not. A change of any consequence may need its clinical safety case revisited, its hazards reassessed, its validation repeated; and it lands not on one cloud tenant you control but on dozens of trusts running their own versions on their own infrastructure, frequently with their own UAT systems, each with its own change board and its own appetite for risk. The sector is barely touched by the software-as-a-service model that makes continuous delivery painless elsewhere. So the bottleneck does not vanish. It moves, decisively, from the part the machine has just made cheap to the part it cannot touch: deciding whether a change is safe, and being able to prove it. Which is, if you have been keeping score since Chapter One, the difficult bit. The machines have simply cleared away everything that was distracting us from it.

Proving it's safe has a last step no change board can perform for you, and healthcare is the one corner of software that has never been willing to skip it. The habit clinical vendors tend to treat as friction (that clinicians insist on testing the thing themselves before they will trust it) turns out to be the method's last move rather than an obstacle to it. User acceptance testing is another prototype session. The clinician at go-live saying "not like that" is the haematologist from Chapter Seven, still doing the single most useful thing anyone in the process does, only now at the end of the line instead of the start. The reaction that is the requirement does not stop at the handoff, or the test suite. It runs all the way to the ward, where it is the last line of the safety case as surely as it is the last requirement: the one thing no document can certify on the clinician's behalf. Healthcare's stubbornness about putting a real user in front of the real thing is not the sector being slow. It is the sector being right, and the rest of software may yet come to envy it.

* * *

It is worth, this near the end, saying where the early chapters land. The factory manager from Chapter One, who was never in the room until it was too late, is the reason any of this matters: the whole apparatus exists to get the right reaction in front of the right person early enough for it to be cheap. The specification illusion of Chapter Two, the beautiful document that was admired and bypassed, is what the verifiable abstraction layer finally answers, because a passing acceptance test is a specification that cannot be admired and ignored. The provenance of Chapter Nine, the requirement that carries its story, is what lets a human stand behind work a machine produced. And the partition of Chapter Fourteen, invariant against contingent, is the line the whole team now organises around: the machine takes the contingent and the cheap, the humans keep the invariant and the consequential. None of these chapters was really about software. They were about who gets to be surprised, and when, and how much the surprise costs.

So the shape of the team bends toward the two things that were always hard and are now, very nearly, all that is left: knowing what to build, and being able to show it is acceptably safe. Fewer hands on keyboards, more eyes on consequences. The developer becomes the person who decides what must never happen and verifies that it does not; the tester becomes the person who tries to make the forbidden thing happen anyway; the clinician remains the person who looks at the result and tells you, in one sour question, what you have still not understood; and the clinical safety officer, who was never a stage in any pipeline, does not fold away, because you cannot automate the willingness to be accountable for a life. I do not know whether the teams end up smaller or merely stranger, nor where the next generation of seniors comes from once the gym has closed. This is a gamble, like the two chapters before it, and the sort that is often wrong in the interesting direction. But if it lands even roughly, the people who do well out of it will be the ones who were never really being paid to type, and were always, secretly, being paid to know what should and what should never have been built in the first place.

On a closing note, I've spoken of 'the method' a few times throughout the book, but you could just as easily call it 'the approach'. I don't have a name for it. I'm a great believer in nominative determinism, so I think naming it would be foolhardy at best, and I certainly don't want to own it. I suspect a lot of it is already out there anyway. I prefer to think of it more as a way of thinking and coming at problems that I've learned the hard way and, as my karate teacher likes to remind me: "A fool never learns. A smart man learns from his mistakes. A wise man learns from the mistakes of others". To be fair, he's usually saying this to our lower belts as I land on the floor, but he's not wrong.

Part Five: The Playbooks

Appendix A: What can be done today

The method of this book, compressed into something you can run today.

How to use this Playbook

Throughout this book I've done my best to make a case for rapid prototyping, using modern AI tools that can produce fully working interfaces and applications cheaply enough, and at sufficient pace, for them to be a viable discovery tool. Now, it's time for me to walk the walk, or eat my own cat food, or some such tomfoolery.

This is the part you can keep open on the desk while you act on it, like a recipe. Everything here is a compression of the method the chapters argued for, turned into something you can follow on a Monday morning without re-reading fifteen chapters: the loop that runs from 'a problem to solve' or a desired outcome, via a vague idea and a conversation, to production-grade intent software whose safety you can actually make the case for. Where the chapters build their ideas slowly, with stories, the Playbook states them quickly.

This is Appendix A: the method as you can run it now, with today's tools and a real handoff still in it. Appendix B takes the identical module and asks what changes if the cost of building collapses the way Chapters Fourteen to Sixteen propose it will, is already doing even. Same problem, two timelines; read this one first.

One example runs through the whole thing, because a method is easier to trust when you have watched it work once, end to end, than when it is described in the abstract, and I have run this one in real life. The example is the sample collection module from Chapter Eight: the system a phlebotomist uses to manage a blood draw across one or more orders for the same patient. It earns its place twice over. It is clinically real, with genuine consequences if it is wrong (the right label on the right tube for the right patient is not a nicety), and it is the one whose early screens, shown too soon, nearly became a promise before they were a product, and then became an excellent product because the right people reacted to them.

I've filled in worked examples as a notepad rather than a form. Treat them as exactly that, worked examples and not gospel: your envelope, your personas and your hazards are yours to discover, in whatever shape suits you, which is rather the point.

One caution about the shape of what follows. The notepads and checklists are the residue of the method, not the method itself. Each one is what a conversation leaves behind once it has done its work: the envelope is what you pre-decided, the persona notes are who you met, the provenance is what was said and why. Filling them in is not the activity; having the exchange that fills them is. If you can complete every notepad without anyone, or anything, wincing at a screen, you've built a filing system rather than a product. The point of the method has always been the reaction, and the reaction comes only from a real exchange, increasingly one that now includes the machine itself as a participant rather than a tool (see Stage Two, where it dons a persona before the room does).

A note on how I hold all this together, before we begin. Everything that follows has to be captured somehow, but, as I said, I'm not going to hand you a stack of forms and call that the method. There is nothing blank at the end to fill in. What follows tells you what has to survive each stage, and how to draw it out of whoever, or whatever, you're getting it from. The shape you record it in is yours.

There's a deeper reason to keep this loose. The old instinct was to formalise early: to take a messy human intention and carve it into a Business Requirements Document; precise, numbered, signed off, and (as Chapter Two showed) admired and then promptly ignored. That asked people to be rigorous far too soon, and about exactly the thing they're worst at. We're good at ambiguity, context and the half-formed 'not like that'; we're terrible at premature precision. Another one of my favourite bits of the Agile approach is not making decisions until you need to, this is in that vein, so don't formalise here. Capture the goals and objectives in context, in whatever loose shape holds them, and leave the formal artefact for later, and for the one participant that's actually good at formality. The rigour crystallises out in the Gherkin of Stage Five like a precipitate coming out of solution, and it's largely written by the machine, because turning a well-understood intention into exhaustive, formal Given/When/Then is precisely what a machine does better than any tired human with a template. People supply the indeterminism; the machine supplies the formalism. It's the right way round, at last.

I'm showing you mine because a worked example is easier to trust than a principle, but please treat it as exactly that. The way I tend to hold a problem together is a plain flow diagram with the requirements, the user stories, hung off the boxes. Nothing clever: start and stop ovals, squares for the actions, diamonds for the decisions, the odd callout or a little cylinder where some data is doing more work than it lets on. No particular flavour, and only the occasional swim-lane when 'who' is important.

I've used the grown-up notations, UML, BPMN, the towering edifice that is TOGAF, and they all have their place, but the moment a notation makes you stop and wonder whether you've drawn the arrowhead correctly, it's started charging rent on the very attention you came here to spend on thinking. The basic flowchart earns its keep precisely because it's open and interpretable enough to be wrong in comfort: you can sketch it on a whiteboard, get it half right, and let someone who knows better jab a finger at the box in the wrong place.

And there's a plainer reason still, the one that actually clinches it. A diagram is only worth drawing if everyone who has to react to it can read it, and a formal notation fails that test the moment the room is mixed. Hand a BPMN model to a phlebotomist, or a UML class diagram to a clinical safety officer, and you haven't communicated, you've set an exam. The whole method runs on reaction (Chapter Six's room, Chapter Seven's wince), and people can only react to what they can read. In my time I have never once met anyone, clinician, manager, developer or thoroughly nervous stakeholder, who couldn't read an old-fashioned flowchart. Boxes are things, diamonds are choices, arrows are what happens next: that's the whole syntax. The machine reads it happily too, which is a bonus most complex notations can't credibly claim to beat without putting their creator in a straightjacket.

So: this is my way of capturing things. I learned the basics at school, drawing boxes and diamonds for some long-forgotten exercise, and they've been in my toolkit ever since. You use whatever works for you. This isn't another documentation standard trying to join the pile; it's a way of aiding proper thinking, and the only test it has to pass is whether it helps the right person see the wrong thing in time to say so.

Stage One: Draw the envelope first

Before you provoke a single reaction, write down the part you already know. Chapter Fourteen split requirements into two kinds: invariant, which describe how the thing is built, and contingent, which describe what it does for the people who use it. The contingent part is the rest of this Playbook; you discover it. The invariant part you can write down in advance, and you should, because it is the cheapest thing you will do all project and it is what lets everything after it move fast without falling over. The invariant set itself comes in two layers, and it pays to keep them apart: the platform, which is how anything gets built at all and is much the same whatever you are building, and the non-functional requirements, which are how this particular thing must behave. The first you pre-load and forget; the second, as we'll see, the prototype actually helps you pin down.

The platform: how anything gets built

Capture the invariant set once and write it down as standing constraints rather than as a document that gets admired and ignored (Chapter Two): this is the architecture, these are the patterns and the coding standards we treat as best practice, this is the language, SDK and framework we build on, here is what 'tested' means, here is what we will never do to a patient's data. You can hand that file to your AI collaborator today, and people do. What it buys you now is a prototype built on a fixed frame instead of on sand, and an eventual build with a clear target to hit. (Appendix B asks what happens when the same envelope lets the prototype itself grow into the product. Here we keep the more familiar shape, where the prototype is still a prototype and there is a real handoff to come.)

A distinction that matters more in clinical software than almost anywhere: not all invariants are equally permanent. Some are yours (your architecture, your naming, your logging) and you can revise them whenever you like. Others are borrowed: external standards you do not own and cannot change, only follow. These are invariant in the sense that you must obey them, but only temporarily, because the body that issued them can revise them without asking you. The order in which blood tubes must be drawn (blood cultures, then light-blue citrate, then serum, then green heparin, then lavender EDTA, then grey fluoride or oxalate) is a standard, not a preference; get it wrong (and I may have just done that, local lab guidance should be followed because colours/additives can vary) and one tube's additive contaminates the next and the tests fail. It is about as invariant as a clinical rule gets. And yet, while this book was being written, the relevant standard changed its name and edition, from CLSI GP41 to CLSI PRE02 (8th edition, 2025). The rule barely moved; the reference did.

So a borrowed invariant goes into the envelope differently from a house one: pinned to its issuing body, its version and its date, with a standing trigger to re-check it when a new edition lands. An invariant you do not own is a subscription, not a possession.

One thing the envelope is not is a safety guarantee. You can preload the standards and the generic guardrails, but as Chapters Eleven and Fourteen both warn, what counts as a hazard is discovered by reaction like everything else, so the safety case is assembled later (Stage Eight), not declared here. The envelope makes the build sound. It does not make it safe on your behalf.

For the sample collection module, the envelope looks roughly like this.

Envelope element	*What it pins down*	*Sample collection module*
Language, SDK & best practice	*The stack you build on and the coding standards you hold to*	*The company's platform stack and component library; approved dependencies only; the team's coding standards and agreed patterns, handed to the AI as the rails it builds inside*

		(Chapters Thirteen to Fifteen)
Architecture & patterns	*The structural decisions every feature must obey*	*Every draw action is an immutable, audited event; label, tube and patient are bound at the moment of printing and cannot be silently reassigned*
Security & privacy	*How patient-identifiable data is handled*	*PID encrypted at rest and in transit; no PID written to logs; every read of patient data recorded*
Data & interoperability (borrowed)	*The external data standards your data must conform to*	*Orders and results exchanged as HL7 V2.4; pin the version in use and review on each release*
Definition of 'tested'	*What must be true before code is allowed to exist*	*Every behaviour has an executable scenario; no scenario, no merge*
Borrowed clinical invariants	*Published standards you must follow, with version and review trigger*	*CLSI PRE02 (8th ed., 2025) order of draw and additive sequencing; DCB0129 clinical-safety process; re-check on each new edition*
House invariants	*Your own conventions, revisable by you*	*Naming, logging format, code-level error handling (how faults are caught and recovered, as opposed to how they are shown to the user), accessibility baseline*

Notepad: the envelope (worked example, sample collection module). Yours will hold different things.

The other half of the envelope: the non-functional requirements

The platform tells you how anything gets built. It says nothing about how this particular thing must behave, and that is the second half of the envelope. These are the non-functional requirements: how fast it must respond, how it speaks to the user when something needs attention (a toast, a timer, a banner, a blocking alert that has to be acknowledged), and the look and interaction it must inherit, whether that is an existing app it is being bolted onto or simply the corporate brand. They are invariant in the sense that you commit to them as targets, but unlike the platform you don't load them once and forget them, because they are notoriously the hardest requirements to make stick.

Part of the reason is that, on paper, a non-functional requirement dissolves in a fog of perfectly reasonable objections as per Chapter Thirteen. This is where the prototype does something a specification never could. It makes the requirement felt rather than argued: nobody debates whether speed matters once they have used the two-second version and the three-hundred-millisecond version one after the other. And it is an existence proof, which is a far harder thing to wave away than a target nobody has yet hit: it can be done, here it is doing it. It is also where the requirements you would never have thought to write down surface on their own: that the mismatch alert has to be loud enough to stop a tired hand, that the whole thing has to work one-handed and in gloves, the things a phlebotomist discovers for you the moment the prototype is in their actual hand (Chapter Seven).

There is a second reason non-functionals are slippery, and it is the more interesting one: many non-functional requirements are subjective. They don't have a single correct value, only a value that depends on whose hand the system is in and what that person is doing. A phlebotomist with a needle in someone's arm needs to mark a tube collected with one finger, instantly, or they will simply stop using the thing; the clerk running a subject access request that takes two minutes to assemble a whole record doesn't care about the wait, as long as it shows progress so they can get on with something else, or treat it as a sanctioned excuse for a coffee. Same kind of requirement, opposite targets. So you don't specify a number and impose it everywhere; you specify it per persona, and the prototype with its cast (Stage Three, Chapter Ten) is precisely how you calibrate it. The global 'under 500ms for everything' is what you write when you haven't asked whose 500ms it is, which is why it satisfies nobody and gets dropped without argument.

Not every non-functional requirement gets a vote, though, and the difference matters. An OWASP vulnerability is not subjective; no persona's convenience is allowed to lower the bar, however much it would speed their day. That is the tell for which half of the envelope a requirement belongs in. If someone's preference may legitimately move it, it is a subjective NFR, calibrated per persona and discovered by reaction. If no one's convenience may ever move it (security, patient-identity integrity, the order of draw), it is platform, and it is absolute. Subjective never means optional; it means the target is set by the hand it is in, not that there isn't one.

One honesty, so this isn't oversold. A prototype's snappiness is not the production system's snappiness. A prototype on local data with a single user proves that the target is meaningful and the experience is right; it does not prove the system will hold that target under real load. That guarantee is the job of the platform half, the architecture you chose precisely so that three hundred milliseconds survives a thousand users. So the two halves hand off to each other: the non-functional layer sets and validates the target by reaction, and the platform layer is how you actually keep it. The developer's 'but what about concurrency' is not obstruction; it is the honest seam between the thing the prototype proved and the thing the build still has to earn.

For the sample collection module, the non-functional half of the envelope looks roughly like this.

Non-functional requirement	*What it pins down*	*Sample collection module*
Response & feedback time	*How quickly it must respond, and what the user sees while it works*	*Persona-relative, not one flat number: instant for the phlebotomist mid-draw (mark a tube collected with one finger, acknowledged within 100ms) or they stop using it; a slower, progress-showing view is fine for end-of-shift batch review. Set the target by the hand it is in*
Alerting & error surfacing	*How the system tells the user something needs attention (distinct from how the code handles the fault)*	*A patient or tube mismatch is a blocking alert that must be acknowledged to proceed, never a toast that can scroll away; transient issues such as a busy printer are non-blocking and self-clearing*
UI/UX conformance	*The look and interaction it must inherit*	*Matches the existing ward app's components, type scale and colour roles; introduces no new navigation a phlebotomist has to learn mid-shift*

Notepad: the non-functional requirements.

Stage Two: Get it off the ground

The introduction to this Playbook promised a loop that runs from a vague idea, through a conversation, to working software, and then the stages rather skipped the conversation. Here it is. Before there is anything to react to, there has to be a first runnable thing, and the cheapest way to get one is to describe what you want and let the machine build it. This is the step where the prototype is born, and it is a conversation, not a form.

To make that concrete, here's how the sample-collection harness actually got off the ground, because the principle is the easy part and the cold start is where people freeze. I began by asking my engineers and then telling the machine what we build on: the SDK, the versions, the shape of our stack, none of which I could have configured unaided, because I'm a capable analyst and a thoroughly rusty developer (the last environment I set up by hand has since been quietly retired, possibly out of embarrassment). It walked me through the lot, install this, run that, here's why the toolchain is sulking, now stand up a local SQL Server instance and point it here. Then I handed it the materials the earlier stages had produced, the personas and the aims for them and the module, and told it to build inside them. Within a day I had a working platform, and by the end of the next the conversation had gone from 'here's our platform and here's who this is for' to something a phlebotomist could actually click, not because I'd become a developer overnight but because I'd stopped needing to be one to get a first wrong thing built.

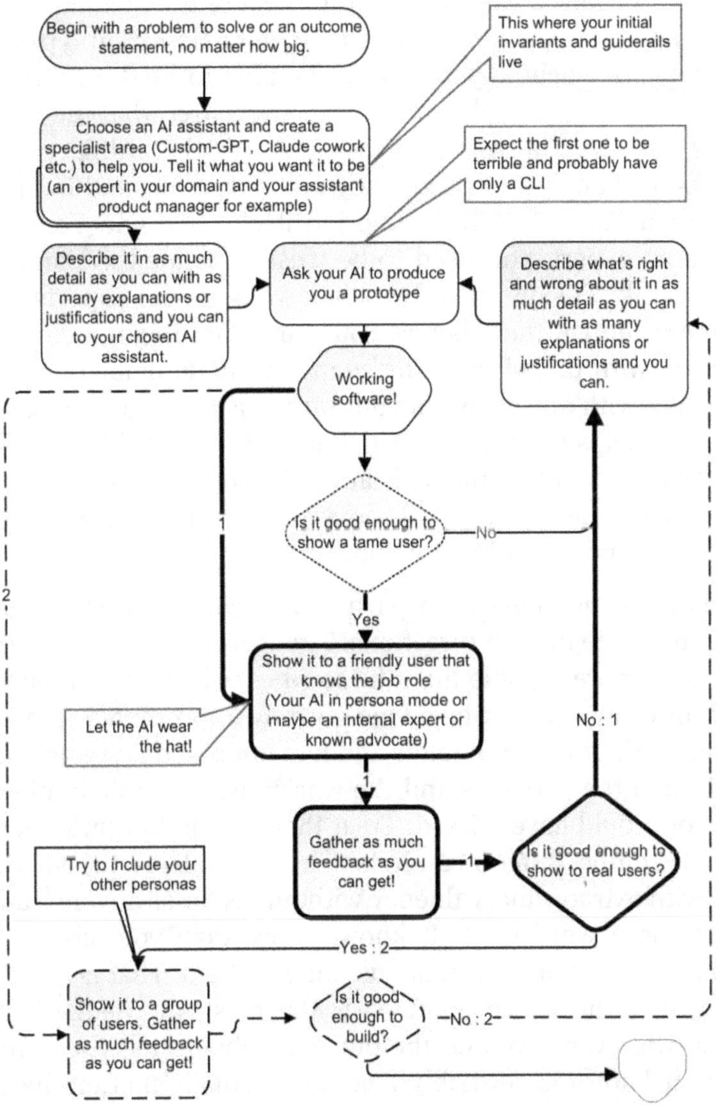

The whole loop, build to first sign-off.

Before any of this, a word about you, because the method assumes something about the person running it. To get a first prototype off the ground with the machine you have to be able to hold an intelligent conversation about the problem: who the users are, what they are for, what the rules are. That is not a high bar, it is the ordinary competence a business analyst or product owner is paid for, and I am going to assume you have it, because the job itself entails it. You do not need to be an expert; you need to be trusted, treated as competent, and able to talk sensibly with the people who are the experts. If you are not there yet, get there before you start. That might mean a long conversation with the AI until the shape of the domain comes clear, or a day spent with one or two of your target users (I have done exactly that, and it helps both sides more than you would think), or simply sitting down and reading the legislation. Whichever it is, there is no free lunch here: the machine will do a great deal of the work, but it will not do the understanding for you.

Which brings me to the other party to that conversation, because it is easy to misjudge in both directions. The machine you are prototyping with is far more capable than the sceptics will tell you. It surfaced the order-of-draw rule in Stage One entirely unprompted, a piece of clinical sequencing I did not know and had not asked for; give it a role and it will find the personas and the workflows that role implies, often ones you would have missed. Treat that as real. But underneath it is still a reasoning difference engine: it manipulates the shapes of meaning with extraordinary fluency without, as far as anyone can tell, understanding a word of it. It knows more than you, about more things than you, and it comprehends none of them. That is not a contradiction, it is the whole point. It is the most knowledgeable colleague you will ever have and the one least able to tell you which of the things it knows is verifiably true, and actually matters here. So you bring the judgement and the stakes, it brings the breadth and the recall, and neither of you is doing the other's job.

Mine usually starts with a single sentence. For the sample collection module it might have been: 'I need an easy-to-use interface that lets a phlebotomist complete blood draws as safely and efficiently as possible while they are actually performing the venepuncture.' That sentence is doing more than it looks. It names the persona (a phlebotomist), the outcome (safe, efficient draws), and, in its final clause, the hardest situation of the lot: hands busy, needle in an arm, which is the live response class from Stage One that settles half the non-functional requirements before anyone has typed a line.

From there the machine does what a useful collaborator does: it asks the questions the sentence left open (one patient, or several orders at once? what happens when a tube is missed?), proposes a first shape, makes a few reasonable default choices, and stands up something you can click. It builds inside the Stage One envelope, so the first harness sits on the platform's rails rather than on sand. (I typically get Claude Code to work mine up into a passable UI, mainly because I'm too lazy and out of date to write the code.) Sometimes the more useful output of the conversation isn't the application at all but a precise prompt for the tool that will build it. Either way the conversation has done its job, because what it produces is a thing the next two reactions can bite on.

One discipline, and it is the same one this very module had to learn the hard way (Chapter Nine). The first harness is seductive precisely because it looks finished, and the temptation is to take it to a stakeholder and let them admire it. Don't. It is scaffolding built to provoke a reaction, not a demo built to sell, and every tidy default it chose is a decision nobody has signed off yet, bound for Stage Four. Get it off the ground, then break it on purpose: the point of building it quickly is to find out quickly how it's wrong.

First, let the machine wear the hat

One more move belongs here, and the diagram's callout on it says the essential thing: let the AI wear the hat before a real person does, asking it to react in persona as the paediatric phlebotomist or the lab scientist. Treat what it says as a hypothesis to check, not a sign-off, it can be confidently wrong in exactly the register that makes you believe it (Chapter Fourteen's mis-partition). The order-of-draw rule in Stage One arrived this way, unprompted, and this time correct; the next one it offers with equal confidence may not be.

Stage Three: Run the prototype session

Now you go and discover the contingent part, and the only way to do that is to provoke a reaction. Build something whole enough to react to (Chapter Five): real screens, a real flow, not a collection of boxes on a diagram. Then show it to the people who actually do the work, and resist the urge to present it. You are not selling; you are fishing for the sour note. Remember, the most useful sentence in the whole method is still some version of 'why would it do it like that?'

Get the right people in the room, and remember the difference between direct experience and observed reaction (Chapter Seven): you can play at being a phlebotomist for an afternoon, but the years of tacit knowledge live in a person who can spot a juicy vein at 20 feet. When the reaction comes, transcribe it, do not paraphrase it. The phlebotomist who tells you they keep pre-printed tube labels stuck up their arm because the old system used a laser printer has just handed you a requirement and a hazard in one sentence; write it down in their words, not yours.

The cast you bring, and keep (your personas)

Persona	Situation	What changes their behaviour
Day ward phlebotomist	Routine round, known inpatients	Time to confirm identity; standard order sets; familiar workflow
Paediatric phlebotomist	Neonatal or paediatric ward; volume-critical	Minimising tubes and total volume is paramount; aggregation rules tighten; small veins, fewer attempts, greater chance of failure
A&E phlebotomist	Urgent or critical patients. may need to use emergency/provisional identification workflows	Speed and provisional identity; STAT orders arrive mid-draw. standardised broad orders, preset emergency panels, or rainbow draw protocols
Biomedical scientist (lab)	Downstream; receives the samples, never sees the patient	Rejects mislabelled, mis-ordered or contaminated samples; the last line before a result is reported

Notepad: the personas, the cast you keep.

The diagram's two checkpoints are this cast compressed: the friendly user is your fastest single persona, the group step is where the rest, paediatric, A&E, lab, get their turn.

The session itself

- Show a whole, navigable prototype, not isolated screens.
- Provoke, don't present: ask them to do a real task, even offer an arm for a simulated draw and watch where they wince. (If you wince, re-read and note 'simulated')
- Have each relevant persona react in their own situation (day, paediatric, A&E, lab).
- Transcribe reactions verbatim; capture who said it, in what context, and why.
- Note every change you make in response, so the prototype stays a record of decisions (Stage Four depends on it).

Stage Four: Reverse-engineer the requirements

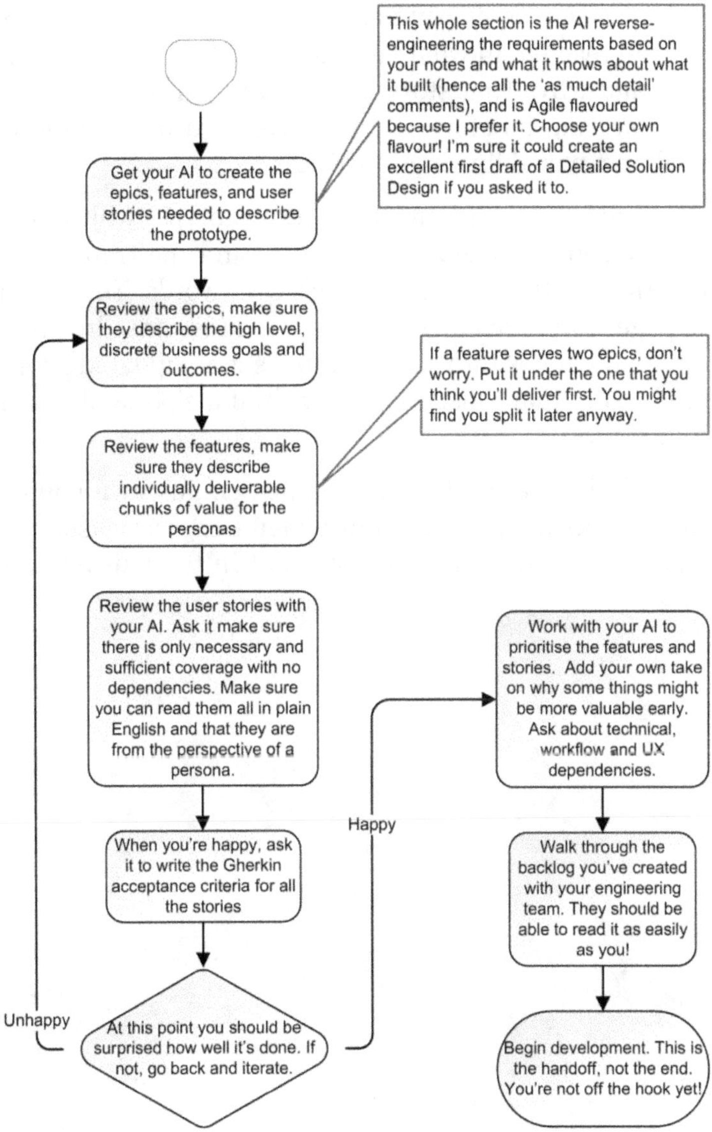

Backlog to handoff, the second half of the loop.

When you sit down to write the requirements, you'll find most of them are already in the prototype, because every feature exists because someone asked for it or reacted to its absence (Chapter Nine). The job isn't to invent requirements but to pull them out and attach their story: who reacted, in what situation, what the system did, what it should do, and why. That story is the thing that has to survive. A requirement carrying its story is far harder to drop unnoticed in a busy sprint than a naked line in a backlog.

It comes from two places, mostly: the prototype, which is now a record of every choice someone reacted to, and the transcript from Stage Three, the reactions in the person's own words. You're not facing a blank page; you're reading back what the sessions already wrote. If it helps, feed the notes into the machine, get an updated prototype, and go round again; that's just good Agile thinking pointed in a slightly different direction.

How you hold it is where I hand you the pen. My own habit is the flow I keep going on about: each requirement hangs as a user story off the box it belongs to, so it lives at the point in the journey where it actually bites.

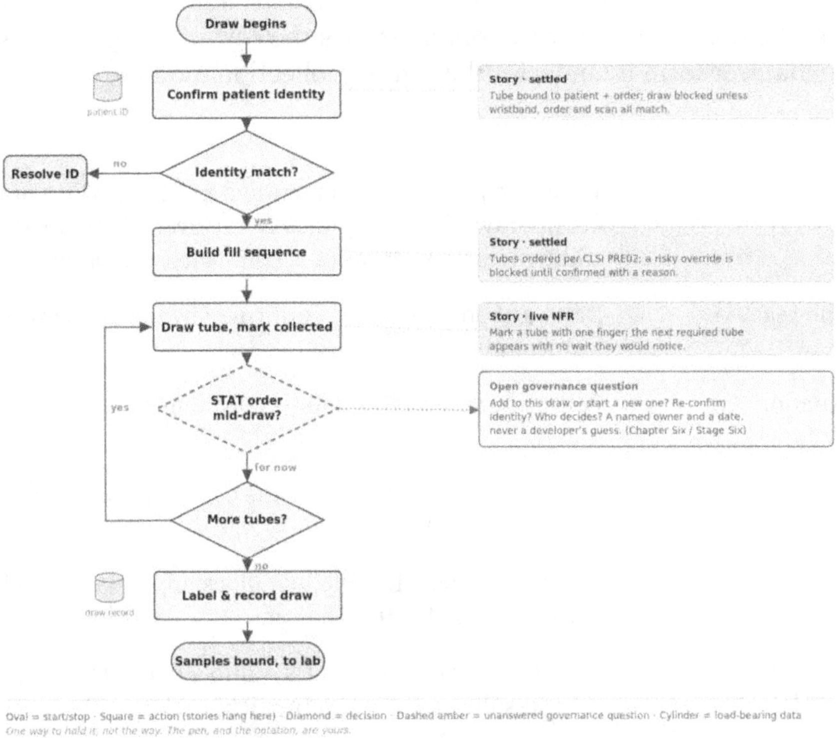

The sample collection flow, with stories on the boxes, the trunk marked as data, and the one unanswered decision flagged rather than guessed. One way to hold it, not 'the' way.

The decisions the build made silently, the ones nobody asked for, show up as a box happily doing something load-bearing with no story attached: in an early phlebotomy build the tool offered the tubes in the order the orders happened to arrive, which is to say in no clinical order at all. Nobody decided that; it simply defaulted. On the flow it's a naked box, which is exactly how you catch it. Surface it, name it, and check it against the clinical intent, because a decision without provenance is the one that gets changed later by someone who never knew it mattered.

The questions you can't answer yet don't get guessed either. They stay on the diagram as open diamonds, each with a named owner and a date, waiting for Stage Six to close them.

If a record per requirement suits you better than a picture, keep one; the point was never the shape. Here's the sort of thing I capture, in whatever form it lands, for the sample collection module:

Field	Entry
Requirement	Tubes are proposed and recorded in CLSI PRE02 order of draw; the system blocks any override that risks additive carryover until it is confirmed with a reason.
Who reacted	Day ward phlebotomist; confirmed by the lab biomedical scientist.
Situation	Collecting several tubes for one patient on a routine round.
What the prototype did	Proposed tubes in the order the orders arrived (effectively arbitrary).
What it should do	Order them per CLSI PRE02; block any risky override until confirmed with a reason.
Why (clinical rationale)	Additive carryover (e.g. EDTA into a later tube) invalidates results and forces a re-stick.
Hazard if wrong	Invalid results acted on, or repeat venepuncture; worse in paediatrics.
Source	Prototype session 2, [date].

Notepad: a requirement with its provenance.

Stage Five: Write the acceptance criteria

Everything up to here was kept deliberately informal: goals and reactions, held in context, in a shape loose enough to think in. This is the one stage that needs to be formal, and so it's the one stage you should largely hand over. Give the AI the requirement and its story and let it draft the Given/When/Then; exhaustive formal constructs are what it's genuinely good at, far better than a person with a template and a spare afternoon. Your job flips from author to editor: the format is easy, and now it's cheap, so the whole of the work is checking that the machine's tidy scenarios say what the sour note actually meant (Chapter Ten).

If the format is easy; the content is the work. Aim for necessary and sufficient coverage: specify the distinctions that change the behaviour and collapse the ones that don't. The personas earn their keep here as guardrails, both for you and for any AI you ask to generate variations: a paediatric phlebotomist and an adult day-ward one may genuinely need different behaviour, so they get different scenarios; two situations that produce the same behaviour get one.

The test of a good acceptance criterion is whether it is specific enough to be wrong in an interesting way. Compare a scenario that cannot fail with one that can.

Not wrong enough to fail:

Given a phlebotomist is collecting samples

When they add tubes to the draw

Then the tubes should be in the right order

Written so it could actually fail:

Given a day ward phlebotomist is collecting multiple tubes for a single patient

When the system builds the recommended fill sequence

Then the tubes are ordered per CLSI PRE02 (blood culture, light-blue citrate, serum, green heparin, lavender EDTA, grey fluoride/oxalate)

And any override into a sequence that risks additive carryover is blocked until confirmed with a reason

Note: e.g. a lithium heparin green-top may be accepted instead of a serum red/gold-top for some routine biochemistry tests, where locally validated.

That 'Note:' might well give rise to another scenario. Or, change the persona and the behaviour legitimately changes too, which is exactly what a second scenario is for:

Given a paediatric phlebotomist is collecting samples for a neonate

When several orders require the same additive type

Then the system aggregates them into the fewest tubes and smallest total volume that still satisfy every order

And it flags when cumulative volume approaches the age- and weight-based limit

Performance is the awkward case, and it earns one example, because it is the requirement people most often write so it can't fail ('the system responds in an acceptable time') and then can't get signed off. The fix is the one from Stage One: don't specify the number, specify the observable outcome for that persona, and let the threshold live underneath as a test tolerance calibrated against the prototype. The same non-functional requirement then resolves two ways for two different hands.

Live, at the needle:

Given a phlebotomist is actively drawing blood
When they mark a tube collected
Then the display updates to show it collected and presents the next required tube, with no wait they would notice

Background, get on with your work:

Given an information manager has requested a full subject access record
When the system can't return it at once
Then it confirms the request is running and shows roughly how long it will take
And it lets them leave it and do other work without losing the result

Neither Then contains a number, so neither invites the argument about milliseconds that sinks performance requirements in review. What 'with no wait they would notice' actually means in this build sits in the test as a tolerance, set from the prototype and revised without reopening the requirement: one behaviour signed off, one number tuned out of sight.

The test for whether an acceptance criterion is good

- Can a tester verify the Then without asking what it means?
- Does it name the persona and situation, not 'a user'?
- Would that persona recognise the expected outcome as correct?
- Is it specific enough to be wrong in an interesting way?

There are a number of ways to make sure acceptance criteria are 'good to go' and it varies by which toolkit, methodology, or SDLC you're using. I happen to like the Agile 'INVEST' framework, but I still only use it as a guideline or a smell-check if one story seems particularly fishy.

Stage Six: Write the tests first

Those scenarios are not documentation to be written up after the build; they are the build's target, written first (Chapter Eleven). Some are settled: the governance is established, the expected behaviour is not a matter of local disagreement, and you can hand them straight to development.

A settled scenario:

Given a phlebotomist has drawn a tube for a specific patient and order

When the label is printed

Then the tube is bound to that patient and that order
And the draw cannot be recorded unless the scanned tube, the patient wristband and the order all match

Others are incomplete, and the incompleteness is the information. When you cannot complete the 'Then', you have not found a gap in BDD; you have found a governance question nobody has answered yet.

An incomplete scenario:

Given a phlebotomist is midway through a multi-tube draw

When a new STAT order arrives for the same patient

Then ... (add it to the current draw, or start a new one? re-confirm identity? who decides?)

Do not let a developer guess that 'Then'. Log it as a governance question with a named owner and a decision date, take it back to the clinical stakeholders who can answer it, and only then turn it into a scenario. That is the prototype approach working just-in-time: show the incomplete thing to the people who know, and let their reaction complete it.

Stage Seven: Hand it over without losing the thread

In the method as it stands today, there is a real handoff: developers take the prototype, the requirements and the scenarios, and build the production system. The danger is the chain breaking (Chapter Twelve). A developer sees software, not the history of its choices, and the results display that orders by collection time looks, from the outside, like a sort order rather than a clinically load-bearing decision. They may well 'improve' it, reasonably, and never know what they changed.

What protects against that is provenance carried across the handoff, plus an explicit list of the decisions that look cosmetic but are clinical. Keep your own hands on the trunk (the patient-identity binding, the draw-order rule, the paediatric volume limits) and you can let the machine or a junior take the leaves (the convenience features nothing else depends on). Verify at a layer you can check, the passing scenarios and the product behaving as a phlebotomist needs, rather than pretending that reading every line is control.

What the development team must inherit

- The prototype itself, runnable.
- The requirements, each with its provenance record.
- The executable scenario suite: settled scenarios passing, incomplete ones flagged as open governance questions. (Note here that, just like in Agile, it's OK to start work before you know everything, it's going to change anyway.)
- The load-bearing list: the decisions that look cosmetic but are clinical (draw order, label binding, aggregation limits), marked do-not-change-without-review.
- The envelope from Stage One, as the standing constraints the build must obey.

Stage Eight: Build the safety case

Clinical software has to do more than work; it has to be shown to be safe (Chapter Eleven). The chain you have built, reaction to requirement to scenario to passing test to code, is an unusually legible clinical safety artefact, because a clinical safety officer can follow it without assistance. I know this because I have gone through it with both CSOs and FDA Auditors. (If you think a UK hazard log is challenging, the US FDA are federal agents and they do NOT mess about. The approach discussed here actually made one smile, which is, apparently, almost a disciplinary offence.) Map your hazards to this chain. Crucially, the hazards themselves are discovered by reaction, the same way everything else was: you cannot pre-load the ones you have not met yet (Chapter Fourteen).

And the method has one move left, at the very end of the line. User acceptance testing is another prototype session: a real phlebotomist, in their real situation, in front of the real thing. The clinician at go-live saying 'not like that' is the same reaction that started the whole process, only now it is the last chance to catch something before a patient is on the other end of it. Feed any such reaction back through Stages Four to Six before you call it done, and remember to tell them to try to break it.

The hazards, traced:

Hazard	Cause	Mitigation	Evidenced by
Wrong-patient result	Tube mislabelled or misbound	Label binds tube, patient and order; mismatch blocks recording	Settled label-binding scenario and its passing test
Invalid result or repeat stick	Wrong draw order; additive carryover	Enforce CLSI order; block risky override until confirmed	Draw-order scenario and test
Iatrogenic anaemia (paediatric)	Over-drawing total volume	Aggregate to fewest tubes and least volume; flag near the limit	Paediatric aggregation scenario and test

Notepad: the hazards, traced to evidence.

Run UAT as the last prototype session

- Put the real product in front of a real phlebotomist for each persona and situation, on realistic data.
- Watch for the 'not like that' reaction and treat it as a late requirement, not a complaint.
- Feed any reaction back through Stages Four to Six before go-live.
- Record clinical sign-off as part of the DCB0129 (manufacture) and DCB0160 (deployment) safety case.

What has to survive

No blank templates, then. What matters isn't the shape of the record but that a few things survive the journey, in whatever form you keep them: the envelope you settled, the people you met and what changes their behaviour, each requirement with the story of who reacted and why, and the hazards with the evidence that each is handled. The checklists in Stages Five, Seven and Eight are already generic enough to lift as they stand. Honestly, I've kept this as lightweight as I can, because there are rafts of excellent templates for each of these already out there in the worlds of business analysis, requirements engineering, Agile training, TOGAF (if you've got time) and more. I have no desire to re-invent the wheel or pretend to be any sort of guru. If you want a form, find one that works for you and use the hell out of it. Treat the whole method as a touchstone to make sure you're not losing anything, understand what you'd be dropping if you are (you may not need it), and add to mine if you think I've been remiss. Be careful of over-egging the pudding though; remember, Agile got a lot right, and the Agile Manifesto's four values are still relevant:

- Individuals and interactions over processes and tools
- Working software over comprehensive documentation
- Customer collaboration over contract negotiation
- Responding to change over following a plan

The whole loop on a page

- Draw the envelope: the invariants, house and borrowed (borrowed ones pinned to a version and a review date).

  Get it off the ground: turn the one-line idea into a first runnable harness inside the envelope, then let the machine wear the persona and bruise it before a real person does.
- Run the prototype session: provoke a reaction from the right cast, in their real situations, and transcribe it.
- Reverse-engineer the requirements with provenance, and surface the decisions made silently.
- Write the acceptance criteria: Given/When/Then, necessary and sufficient, personas as guardrails.
- Write the tests first: settled scenarios now; incomplete Thens become governance questions to answer before code.
- Hand over without losing the thread: provenance, the load-bearing list, your hands on the trunk.
- Build the safety case (as your context requires).

Appendix B: The Convergence Timeline

The same module, on the timeline where building is nearly free.

Appendix A ran the method as you can run it when I wrote it, with a real handoff still in it. This is the same phlebotomy module on the other timeline, the one Chapters Fourteen to Sixteen wager is already arriving: where the cost of building has collapsed far enough that the prototype and the product stop being two separate things. Read Appendix A first. This only makes sense as a set of differences from it, and I'm not going to re-run all eight stages when only some of them change.

A warning I owe you up front, the same one Chapters Fourteen to Sixteen carried: this is informed speculation, not a report from the far side. I've watched the early part of it happen and I'm extrapolating the rest, which is a polite way of saying guessing, with references. Keep one eyebrow raised throughout.

Here's what changes, before we look at where. In Appendix A the prototype is a question you throw away once it's been answered, and a team then builds the real thing from the answer. On this timeline the prototype is never thrown away, because it was production-grade intent from its first keystroke, built inside the same invariant envelope the real thing would have had to obey. The disposable thing and the permanent thing are the same artefact, grown up rather than rebuilt. Nothing about discovering what to build changes at all. Everything about what happens to the discovery afterwards does.

Stage One: the envelope becomes the spine

Stage One is where the weight lands, because on this timeline the envelope is doing a different job. In Appendix A you create the envelope to give the prototype a fixed frame to sit on and the later build a clear target to hit. Here there is no later build, so the envelope stops being scaffolding and becomes the spine of the thing that ships. You pre-load it once, the platform, the non-functional targets, the definition of tested, the security posture, the borrowed clinical invariants, as standing constraints the machine must obey on every line it writes, and then the prototype grows up inside them instead of being rebuilt to meet them afterwards.

The mechanics of drawing it don't change. House invariants are still yours to revise; borrowed ones are still a subscription rather than a possession, pinned to a version and a review date (CLSI PRE02 will have another edition along in due course, and the trigger to re-check it matters more when the system obeys it directly rather than through a developer who might happen to notice). What changes is the consequence of getting it wrong. In Appendix A, a thin envelope gives you a wobbly prototype and a painful build. Here a thin envelope ships. Everything you failed to make invariant, the system is free to get wrong at production scale, without fuss, for as long as nobody reacts to it.

Which sharpens the oldest warning in this book to a point. The envelope is powerful precisely because it's fixed, and dangerous for exactly the same reason: whatever you declare invariant, you've decided not to discover. Draw it too wide and you've pre-committed to the wrong thing with excellent test coverage, the factory manager's objection foreclosed before he's even in the room (Chapter Fourteen). Draw it too narrow and you've left the load-bearing parts to chance. The envelope was always a judgement. On this timeline it's <u>the</u> judgement. And, as per the 1793 decree made by the French National Convention, "They must consider that great responsibility follows inseparably from great power." (I know, everyone thinks it was Spider-man's uncle Ben)

Stages Two to Five: discovery doesn't change, and that's the point

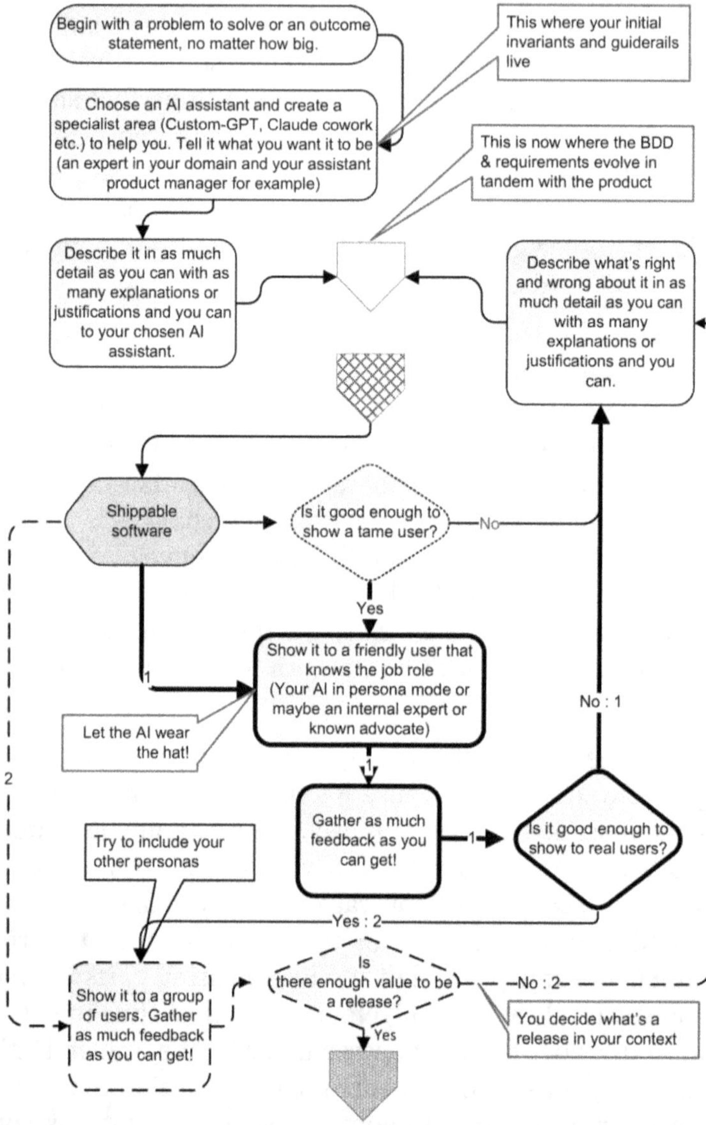

The discovery loop, unchanged from Appendix A. Its old 'good enough to build' gate is now 'is there enough value to be a release', same judgement, renamed for a timeline where the next step might actually be shipping.

Now the anticlimax, and I want it to be one. Getting it off the ground, running the session, reverse-engineering the requirements, writing the acceptance criteria: read Appendix A, because almost none of it moves. The phlebotomist still needs to mark a tube one-handed, still keeps labels stuck up their arm, still looks at the screen and asks why it would do it like that. You still hang the stories off the boxes of a flow anyone in the room can read. The STAT order arriving mid-draw is still a diamond nobody has answered, still a governance question with an owner and a date, not a thing the machine gets to decide because it happened to feel confident.

This is the part of the bet I'm most sure of, because it isn't really a bet. The claim that you discover the contingent part by reaction is a statement about people and problems, not about tools, and no amount of cheap building touches it. If anything the discovery gets more honest, because the thing you're reacting to is already production-grade, so there's less distance between what's built and what's needed. The one thing that gets harder is resisting the temptation to skip the reaction, because a prototype that was always seductive when it looked finished (Chapter Nine) is more seductive still when it genuinely is finished. Show it to the people who know anyway. Watch them wince anyway. The machine being able to build it is not the machine knowing whether it should.

Stage Seven: the handoff inverts

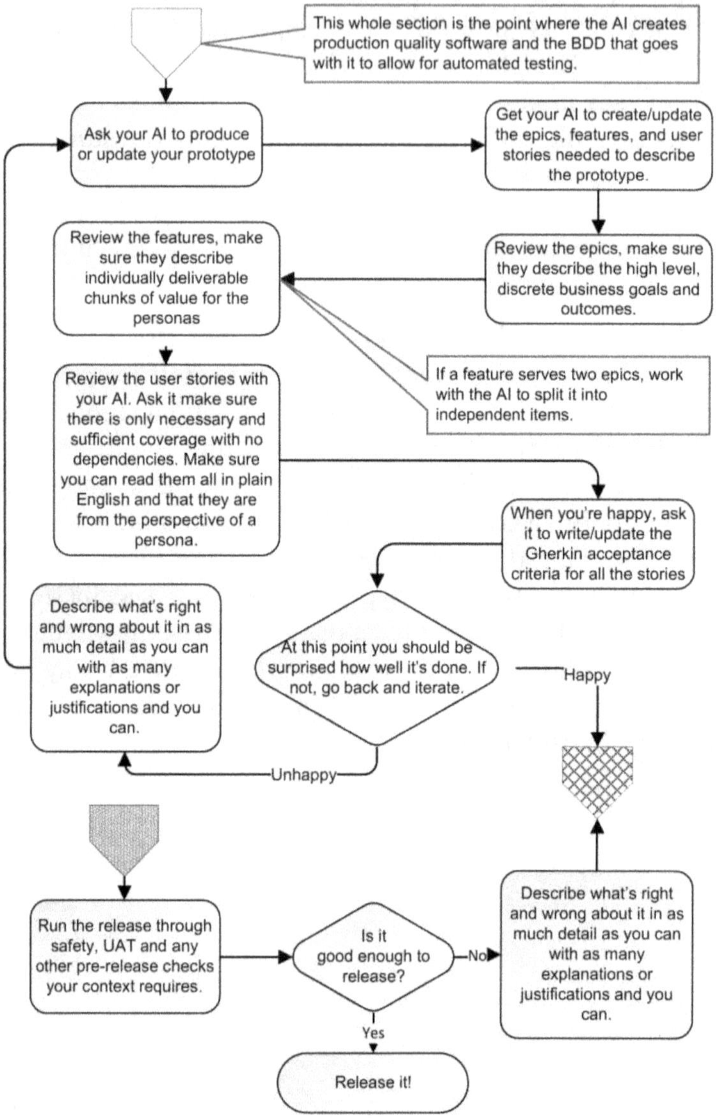

Construction fused with discovery, running all the way to an actual release. The safety and UAT stretch near the end is Stage Eight's subject, arriving here under its own name.

This is the stage that changes shape rather than detail, and it's the whole reason the appendix exists. In Appendix A, Stage Seven is the handoff: developers take the prototype, the requirements and the scenarios, and build the production system, and the danger is the chain breaking, a clinically load-bearing decision mistaken for a sort order and reasonably improved away (Chapter Twelve). On this timeline that handoff doesn't happen at the end, because there's no separate build for it to happen into. It happens at the start, and it's a handoff to the envelope, not to a team.

So the work of Stage Four doesn't disappear, it moves. You still reverse-engineer the requirements out of the reactions, but you do it to feed the standing constraints the system grows inside, not to brief a developer who'll rebuild the thing from scratch. The provenance matters as much as it ever did, arguably more, because the person who now signs off the machine's work needs the story of why a thing is the way it is in order to verify it without reading every line (Chapter Fifteen). Keep your hands on the trunk, the patient-identity binding, the draw-order rule, the paediatric volume limits, and let the machine have the leaves.

This is where the non-functional requirements finally get what Chapter Thirteen promised them: delivered by default. The snappy one-finger response and the blocking identity check weren't bolted onto a finished system and hoped for; the prototype had them from its first breath, because they were in the envelope it grew inside. Nobody retrofits a feeling into a machine that already exists. But hold the honesty Chapter Thirteen insisted on: 'delivered by default' is a property of a prototype that actually grows into production, and the risk hasn't vanished, it's moved. In Appendix A you could lose the snap because a developer improved it away. Here you lose it because the envelope never contained it, and nobody reacted to its absence. The stopwatch is still running; it's just pointing at a different failure.

Stage Eight: safety still doesn't come for free

You can see the tidy ending from here, and it's wrong, so I want to close the door on it. The tidy ending says: if the envelope is the spine and you've pre-loaded the standards, then the system grows up not merely working but safe. It doesn't, and clinical software is exactly where the gap bites.

What counts as a hazard is discovered by reaction, the same way everything else in this book is discovered by reaction. The discharge meeting from an earlier chapter is the proof: a safety requirement that didn't exist until the right person, in the right room, reacted to a real situation. DCB0129 is a process for finding and managing context-specific hazards, not a checklist you can load into the envelope and tick. You can pre-load the process and the generic guardrails; you cannot pre-load the hazards you haven't met yet. So even here, with the building nearly free, the safety case is assembled from the same reactions that give you the requirements, and the method's last move is unchanged: user acceptance testing is another prototype session, a real phlebotomist in front of the real thing, and the clinician at go-live saying 'not like that' is the same reaction that started the whole process, doing the single most useful thing anyone does, one last time before a patient is on the other end of it.

That's the bottleneck moving to exactly where Chapter Sixteen said it would. The machine has cleared away the building, which was never the hard part. What's left, standing on its own with nowhere to hide, is deciding what to build and being able to show it's acceptably safe. Healthcare's stubbornness about putting a real user in front of the real thing was never the sector being slow. It was the sector being right, and this is the timeline on which the rest of software comes to envy it.

The bet, kept honest

One separation to end on, because it's the one that keeps this appendix from ageing badly. There are two claims here and they are not the same size. The structural claim, that there are two kinds of requirement and you front-load the invariant and discover the contingent, is true at any level of machine capability whatsoever, because it's a statement about the problem. The capability claim, that the machines are already good enough to make production-grade-at-prototype-speed the ordinary way of working, is a genuine bet, and a shakier one, because observed exponentials have a habit of turning out to be incomplete sigmoids.

So read Appendix B in pencil. If the bet lands, the eight stages of Appendix A collapse into the two that were always difficult, and the rest is the machine's problem. If it doesn't, Appendix A stands exactly as it is, handoff and all, and you've lost nothing by having imagined the other timeline. Same problem, two appendices: one is what you do on a Monday morning now, the other is what the same Monday looks like when building is nearly free. The method doesn't change between them. Its residue shrinks, until almost all that's left is the reaction and the safety case, which is all it ever really was.

www.ingramcontent.com/pod-product-compliance
Lightning Source LLC
LaVergne TN
LVHW010728061126
851857LV00014B/1387
9781066840403